YOU AND YOUR
Cockapoo

David Alderton

THE *Essential* GUIDE

Hubble & Hattie

For more than eighteen years, the folk at Veloce have concentrated their publishing efforts on all-things automotive. Now, in a break with tradition, the company launches a new imprint for a new publishing genre!

The Hubble & Hattie imprint – so-called in memory of two, much-loved West Highland Terriers – will be the home of a range of books that cover all things animal, all produced to the same high quality of content and presentation as our motoring books, and offering the same great value for money.

More titles from Hubble & Hattie

www.hubbleandhattie.com

First published in June 2010 by Veloce Publishing Limited, Veloce House, Parkway Farm Business Park, Middle Farm Way, Poundbury, Dorchester, Dorset, DT1 3AR, England.
Fax 01305 250479/e-mail info@veloce.co.uk/web www.veloce.co.uk or www.velocebooks.com.
ISBN: 978-1-845843-20-5 UPC: 6-36847-04320-9

Contents

Acknowledgements

Many thanks to Marc Henrie for the majority of the photographic content. Special thanks to Mrs J King; dog groomer, Peter Young; Chris Allen MRCVS BVSc and staff at Medivet, Dene Park, London. Nicole Thompson with Otto; Andi Sisodia and Ziggy, plus children Yusmin, Anya and Natasha; Dawn Bates and Zep; Fiona Steane with Darcy and Monty; Pat Westan with American Cocker Nola, Red Poodle Scoobie, and Cockapoo Trixie.

Introduction

Owning a dog can be a source of great pleasure, bringing a new dimension to your life. Dogs can be great companions, and will encourage you to take more exercise; it's even suggested that owning a dog may improve your health by lowering your blood pressure. Dogs have the potential to help you make new friends as well: studies show that dog ownership can be a more effective way of meeting a potential partner than joining a dating agency! Just as with any new relationship, however, you should not rush into choosing a new dog, especially as, with any luck, your canine friend will be part of your daily life for a decade or more.

Before getting a dog, there are a number of issues that must be considered very carefully, not least of which is the expense; owning a dog will have an undeniable impact on your budget in terms of buying food, as well as purchasing equipment ranging from toys to bedding, and even a car guard. There are also veterinary costs to bear in mind, although you can guard against unexpected bills by insuring your pet, but this will, of course, still add to your outgoings. There are other costs to be considered, too, such as routine vaccinations, deworming medication, and neutering.

A dog in the home

Your domestic arrangements also need to be considered carefully. Dogs are social

Cockapoos make wonderful companions, as they are ideal dogs for people of all ages.

Cockapoos love to play; a reflection of their ancestry, as both of the parent breeds have playful characters.

In addition to the cost of food and equipment, there are a number of other considerations – including veterinary costs – to bear in mind when choosing a pet dog.

creatures, and young dogs in particular will become bored very rapidly and may develop behavioural problems if they are left on their own for long periods every day. Furthermore, it will be much harder to house-train a puppy successfully under these circumstances. There may be factors which prevent you from having a dog. Those in rented accommodation may be prohibited from keeping pets – although there are now more enlightened schemes in the UK and elsewhere that permit pets in rented property, subject to the payment of a higher deposit. There are even some private dwellings that have a covenant prohibiting owners from keeping animals.

Dogs in general will not thrive in surroundings without access to a garden, and even if you have a garden, you will need to ensure that it is securely fenced in order to prevent your pet escaping. Furthermore, you need to be prepared for some disruption within the garden, especially with a puppy that may be inclined to dig up and damage plants. The lawn may not escape unscathed, either, particularly if you choose a bitch, because her acidic urine can cause the grass to die back.

The Cockapoo is not a dog you should consider owning unless you have a garden – or ready access to a park or similar open space – where your pet can play and exercise.

Going away when you have a dog is also unlikely to be as straightforward as in the past, although it may be possible to take your pet with you, depending on your destination. If you live in the UK, for example, you can now travel widely through Europe under the Pet Travel Scheme (PETS), with your dog having what has become known as a 'pet passport.' Advance planning to comply with the criteria of this scheme will be essential, however. Travel to and from North America is also included, although the cost of flying your dog across the Atlantic with you under these circumstances for a relatively short vacation is likely to be prohibitive, and you should also consider whether the stress that this will inevitably cause your pet is justified. If you decide against this route, you will need to investigate other care options for when you are away, such as kennelling for your dog.

When it comes to choosing a particular dog, there are many other aspects to consider. Some people prefer not to opt for a purebred dog, believing that mongrels (dogs of no fixed parentage) are likely to be healthier. There is now a third possibility, however, following the rise of what have been dubbed 'designer dogs.' These dogs are the result of crossbreeding between existing recognized breeds, with the aim being to transfer desirable characteristics from both parents to their progeny, with the additional advantage of minimizing any breed weaknesses. The Cockapoo – the result of crossing a Cocker Spaniel with a variety of Poodle – is one of the best known of these newly emerging types of dogs.

Regular daily walks are essential to keep your dog fit, and also to ensure that it does not grow up nervous of contact with other dogs.

Breed background

Crossbreeding between different types of dog is not a new phenomenon, although those who prefer to maintain the distinctive characteristics of their chosen breed have usually frowned upon the activity. Over recent years, however, interest in crossings of this type has grown, partly due to curiosity, but more significantly because the role of dogs in our lives has undergone a dramatic change. No longer are they kept primarily for their original working traits, and often kennelled outdoors, but are instead household companions, and one of the family. As a result, breeders today are seeking to create new, distinctive, friendly companion dogs that will thrive in domestic surroundings.

Poodles, for example, no longer venture into freezing waters to retrieve waterfowl that have been bagged by hunters. Yet the very distinctive, non-shedding coat of the Poodle is a highly desirable feature for many dog owners. The lack of shed hair means that it is easier to keep the domestic environment clean, and neither do you end up with them all over your clothes!

There is also a suggestion that the coat of Poodles is hypoallergenic (non-allergy producing) — although research suggests that allergens may be linked with canine saliva licked onto the coat by the dog, rather than the coat. Nevertheless, the original interest in crossing Poodles with other breeds began with this hypoallergenic property in mind. The aim was to establish a strain of guide dogs that would be suitable for blind people who were allergic to the breeds frequently

Poodles, such as this red Miniature variety, have been widely used in the breeding of so-called 'designer dogs' — including the Cockapoo.

The Labradoodle was the original 'designer dog,' developed with the aim of creating a hypoallergenic breed to serve as a guide dog. It was created from crossbreeding involving Labrador Retrievers and Standard Poodles.

used for this purpose, such as Labrador Retrievers. This led to the creation of what is currently the best known of the 'designer dogs' – the Labrador Retriever-Poodle cross, known as a Labradoodle.

Variations on a theme

The Cockapoo – occasionally written as Cock-a-poo – emerged in the US during the 1950s, but did not begin to become well known until the following decade. The first puppies were the result of unplanned matings, but were so cute that they soon attracted attention. (In fact, similar crosses may have existed in France during the late 1800s.) The two smaller varieties of Poodle – the Miniature and the Toy – have been favoured in such crossings, since they result in puppies that were similar in size to, or even a little smaller than, the other parent, the Cocker Spaniel. The new breed soon began to build an international following, known as the Spoodle in Australia (although this description may be used elsewhere for any type of Spaniel-Poodle cross), and the Cockadoodle in Sweden.

There are variations in the appearance of Cockapoos today, partly because the American variant of the Cocker Spaniel is slightly smaller than the original English form of the breed, and it also has a longer coat. Both these Cocker Spaniel breeds have been crossed with Poodles, however, and both have contributed to the development of the Cockapoo.

The size of Cockapoo puppies will also vary according to the variety of Poodle used in the crossbreeding. Three distinctive size categories of Poodle are recognized: Standard Poodles measure between 15 and 24in (38-60cm) at the withers (the highest part of the shoulder); the mid-sized Miniature Poodle measures from 10 to 15in (25-38cm); and the Toy stands just 6 to

The English Cocker Spaniel has been favoured for the creation of the Cockapoo in Europe, whereas in the US especially, American Cockers have been used more often.

The use of the American Cocker Spaniel has impacted on various aspects of the Cockapoo's appearance, especially coat length.

11in (15-28cm) tall. Moreover, Toy Poodles weigh between 6 and 13lb (3-6kg), whereas a Standard Poodle may tip the scales at 50lb (23kg), and these differences in weight will also be reflected in the resulting Cockapoo puppies.

There is less difference in size and weight between the two Cocker Spaniel bloodlines, so the impact is potentially less significant. English Cocker Spaniels measure between 15 and 16in (38-41 cm), and typically weigh 28 to 32lb (13-14.5kg), with male dogs being slightly larger than bitches. This contrasts with the American Cocker Spaniel, which is generally about 1in (2.5cm) shorter at the withers, and tips the scales at between 24 and 28lb (11-13kg). Nevertheless, Cockapoo lineages derived from both forms of Cocker Spaniel are recognized separately, especially in the US.

Varied offspring

It is vital to appreciate the key difference between the breeding of pedigree dogs as opposed to designer dogs, since this impacts directly on the appearance of Cockapoos. Purebreds have often evolved over the course of centuries, with progeny carefully mated over many generations to reinforce particular traits, such as appearance and size. This is emphatically not the case with Cockapoos as most puppies are simply the result of matings between a Poodle and Cocker Spaniel. There is no standardization, and this will soon be apparent when several puppies have been viewed. You may see a Cockapoo that appeals greatly to you in terms of its appearance, but this does not mean that the next Cockapoo you see will look just the same. The puppies in a litter may each

Did you know?

The American Canine Hybrid Club is a registry organization set up during 1969 in the US to serve as the primary body for all interbreed or mixed-breed crosses. Although some of these crosses are very rare, and not all are especially distinctive – like the Colonial Cocker Spaniel, bred by crossing the American and English forms of this breed – there are now nearly 400 such pairings that have been recognized and named. The generally accepted practice is for both breeds involved in the original cross to be represented in a shortened version of the official name given to their puppies. The Cockapoo name is a typical example, a combination and an abbreviation of Cocker Spaniel and Poodle. At the time of writing, Cocker Spaniels have contributed to the ancestry of some 20 other crosses of this type, besides the Cockapoo itself, whilst Poodles have featured in more than 50 such pairings.

Cockapoo colouring corresponds to that of the parent breeds: this is a male apricot example.

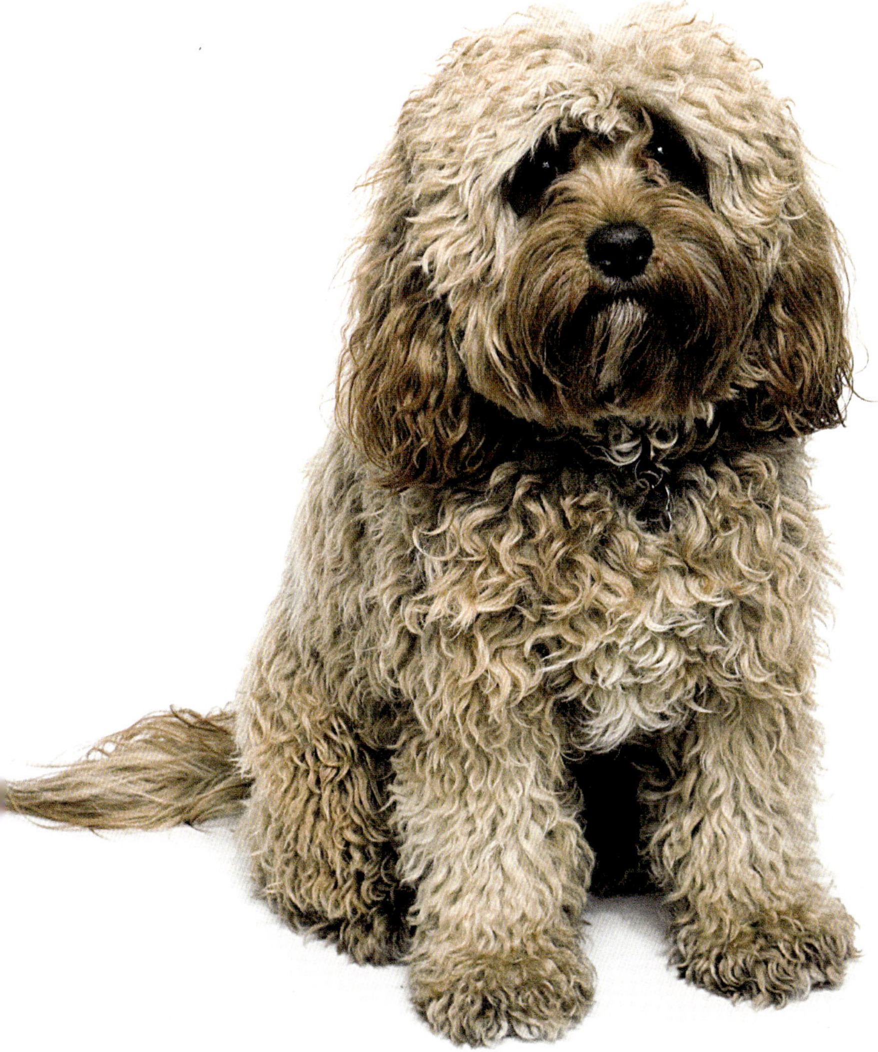

It is difficult to predict the appearance of Cockapoo puppies, particularly from a so-called F1 or first generation cross between a Poodle, such as this white Miniature, and a Cocker Spaniel.

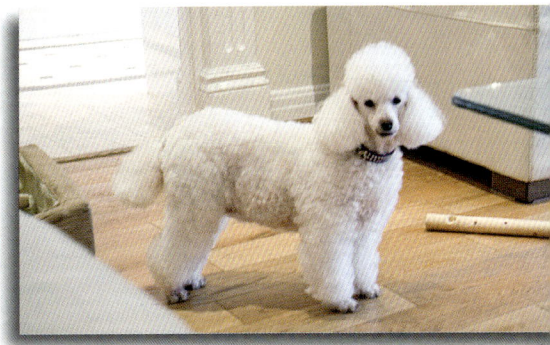

have their own distinctive appearance, with some perhaps resembling one of their parents more than the other, for example.

If you are looking for a Cockapoo with a more consistent appearance, then you will have to seek out puppies from a litter resulting from the mating of two Cockapoos, rather than a Poodle crossed with a Cocker Spaniel. The likelihood is that, genetically, Cockapoos bred from an existing Cockapoo bloodline are more likely to show the distinctive characteristics of such dogs. Certainly in the US, where Cockapoos have existed for over 50 years, there are well-established bloodlines that now produce puppies with a relatively standardized appearance. However, you may simply prefer to have a puppy that will be truly unique, and are not too worried by its appearance.

Colour variations

Poodles incorporate a wide range of colours, which is reflected in the colours of Cockapoos as well. Pale-coloured Cockapoos, including white, cream and silver ones, tend to be popular, as are Cockapoos displaying black coloration. Red, including apricot and various intermediate brownish shades such as sable (which has darker black tipping to the individual hairs), are also seen. Nor do Cockapoos exist in solid colours only; some are bicoloured, with this secondary colouring often extending to the ears. Such patterning is usually quite random, sometimes occurring as a patch over an eye or evident on the underparts.

Even merle coloration may sometimes be seen, in which light and dark hairs mix together to create a mottled pattern. This effect may extend to the feet,

Apricot Cockapoos are often seen, reflecting the fact that this is also a popular colour choice for Poodles, one of the parent breeds.

Bicolours – typically black and white individuals – are common in the case of Cockapoos, with markings that are highly individual.

The black and white colouring in Cockapoos can be traced back to English Cocker Spaniel parents showing the same colours.

causing some toes to appear pinkish, whilst others are dark. Most dramatically, it may affect the eyes, too; these may then take on a dark hue or perhaps be blue, or a combination of both. Particular care needs to be taken with merle pairings, however, since this trait can result in deafness and eye problems. Such dogs must never be allowed to mate together for this reason.

Other genetic considerations

It is often thought that crossbreeds such as Cockapoos are free from genetic weaknesses to which established breeds are susceptible, but this is not the case. The presence of the previously mentioned merle gene is just one example. Each of the Cockapoo's parent breeds have several inherited illnesses in common which could be transmitted to their puppies, and it is therefore important that breeding stock is screened for weaknesses of this type as far as possible.

One of the most serious of these conditions is progressive retinal atrophy (PRA). Signs of the condition will not be apparent in puppies, and obvious symptoms may not even be evident in breeding stock at first, only emerging later in life. A form of PRA described as progressive rod-cone degeneration can afflict both Poodles and Cocker Spaniels. This typically begins as night blindness, with the dog beginning to show signs of the disease when it is between three and five years old. An affected individual may begin to have difficulty seeing objects in its path at night; for example, bumping into chairs in an unlit room, or appearing disorientated if exercised outdoors after dusk.

Ultimately, once the rod cells on the retina (which are responsible for night-time vision) are no longer functioning effectively, the other retinal cells here, known as cones (which facilitate colour and daylight vision), will also begin to fail. By this stage, the dog will start to become blind, and there is no treatment. The genetic problem has been identified on the dog's ninth chromosome, and is known as an autosomal recessive genetic mutation. This means that two dogs may carry the mutation and will not be affected by the illness, whereas, depending how the mutated genes combine when they mate, a percentage of their puppies will be afflicted. This emphasizes the need for screening to eliminate these so-called 'carriers' from breeding programmes.

The other problem from which Cockapoos may suffer is luxating patellas, which is a relatively common condition in smaller dogs, including Miniature and Toy Poodles. In this condition the patella, or kneecap, becomes dislocated, which can cause the young dog to have difficulty walking. This is a congenital problem that the puppy will have had since birth, although, again, this will not be immediately apparent. Both patellas are usually affected, with signs typically becoming apparent in dogs of between four and six months of age.

A veterinary examination and an X-ray of the knee joints will help to assess the severity of the condition, although the extent of the lameness also gives a useful insight. Surgery to stabilize the patellas is usually recommended in more serious cases. It is also important to prevent the dog from becoming overweight later in life, to avoid placing undue strain on this part of the body.

Organizations such as the Cockapoo Club of America (CCA) are encouraging breeders to adopt sensible measures in terms of monitoring breeding stock for these two conditions. Confirmation is requested to show that screening for both PRA and patellar luxation has been carried out before such dogs can be placed on its registry list. This needs to be in the form of an annual Canine Eye Registration Foundation (CERF) examination carried out by a veterinary ophthalmologist to check for PRA, along with certification from the Orthopedic Foundation for Animals (OFA) to show that the dog has no symptoms of patellar luxation. This can be confirmed by a veterinary examination once the dog is at least a year old. Further OFA checks for hip dysplasia and elbow weakness – which can also be genetic in origin – are optional, although neither of these conditions is as common in the Cockapoo's parent breeds.

Points to bear in mind

Although the breeding of Cockapoos in the US is well advanced, with various organizations catering for these dogs, the situation can be quite different elsewhere. In the UK, you are most likely to find puppies resulting from a so-called 'first generation,' or F1 cross, between a Poodle and a Cocker Spaniel, and it is likely to be harder to track down more established strains resulting from Cockapoo-Cockapoo matings. Sometimes, you may see Cockapoo-Poodle or Cockapoo-Cocker Spaniel puppies on offer. In each of these cases, the parental genetic contribution will have a major bearing on the appearance of the puppies. Thus, in the first instance, the Poodle bloodline will predominate, whereas in the second instance, Cocker Spaniel traits will hold sway. Such puppies are therefore more likely to strongly resemble one or other bloodline than will the puppies produced by a Cockapoo-Cockapoo mating.

The likelihood also is that the parents of such dogs will not be of high show standard, but rather of pet-type stock. This is because most breeders are not keen to use their best bitches in breeding projects of this type, preferring instead to use them for maintaining their existing bloodlines. Furthermore, there is no UK breed club at present to oversee and promote the development of the Cockapoo, and nor are these dogs recognized by the Kennel Club.

Even so, it's very important to check that the parents of any puppy you

are thinking of acquiring have been screened for inherited diseases to which the parents are susceptible. No reputable breeder will be offended by your request to see the veterinary certification, but beware if this is not forthcoming: without it, you simply cannot be sure that the genes responsible for inherited diseases have not been passed on to puppies in the litter. Given that Cockapoo puppies often sell for more than either of their parents cost on the basis of their relative scarcity and desirability, this could turn out to be a very expensive gamble, both financially and emotionally.

Personality

One of the best features of the Cockapoo – and which has led to these dogs becoming so popular – is its temperament. Being created from two breeds that are generally enthusiastic, friendly and intelligent means that Cockapoos should also display these traits. The Cockapoo is also highly affectionate towards people in its immediate family group, and learns very rapidly, reflecting the attributes particularly of the Poodle in its ancestry.

Training is quite straightforward, although you will need to concentrate

Like all young dogs,
Cockapoo puppies are
both curious and also
slightly nervous.

One of the
most appealing
aspects of the
Cockapoo is its
very affectionate
nature.

Most Cockapoos love ball chasing games – even if the ball is too big to get in their mouth!

on socializing a young Cockapoo with other dogs, otherwise, you may find that your companion proves to be rather unsociable towards other dogs it meets as it grows up. This socialization can be achieved in part by attending puppy-training classes, as well as by allowing your puppy to mix with friends' dogs once it has completed its initial course of vaccinations. In this way it should learn not to be confrontational from an early age.

While Poodles in general have very stable temperaments, there have been problems in some lines of Cocker Spaniel, which is why it can be so important to see both parent dogs, especially with an F1 cross, so that you can satisfy yourself as far as possible about the nature of both adults.

Cockapoos make excellent family pets, and get on well with children – although you should never leave young children unsupervised with them or, indeed, any other dog. The playful nature of puppies attracts children, but unfortunately, a puppy's claws are potentially much sharper than those of adult dogs because they have not been worn down at the tips. The claws can therefore inflict painful scratches, particularly if the puppy is being picked up incorrectly and feels uncomfortable, causing it to struggle.

Cockapoos are very tolerant with children, which helps explain their growing popularity as family pets.

The Cockapoo coat

As well as body size and shape, the Cockapoo's coat is a significant feature of the breed, and appearance can vary quite widely between individuals, even among littermates. The coat can be relatively straight in some cases, through wavy to even curly, although it should not form kinks. The hair is long and dense, even on the muzzle and legs, and should be trimmed back around the eyes at least, so as not to restrict vision. Cockapoos do not have any lingering 'doggy odour' associated with them, nor do they normally shed their hair over furnishings in the home, so make easy-care companions.

Beware, however, if you are drawn to a Cockapoo on the basis that it won't shed its coat. While this is generally true, it does not always apply and cannot be predicted with certainty when purchasing a puppy: Poodles do not shed but the shedding trait is certainly associated with Cocker Spaniels. Once again, finding a breeder who can offer puppies from a more stabilized Cockapoo bloodline, rather than simply an F1 cross, should enhance the likelihood that the dogs will not moult.

The care of the coat is relatively straightforward, however, irrespective of its type. Simple brushing and combing on a weekly basis should suffice, and you can either clip your Cockapoo yourself, or arrange for this to be carried out

Coat care is not especially demanding, and Cockapoos often seem to enjoy being groomed ...

in a grooming parlour. The coats of Cockapoos are not styled in an elaborate way to resemble those of their Poodle ancestor; instead, they simply require a so-called 'puppy cut,' irrespective of age, which will keep the coat tidy and away from their eyes. It is quite normal for Cockapoo puppies to have shorter coats than adults.

Changing appearance

It is usually possible to predict the size of the puppy from its Poodle ancestry, and smaller Cockapoos tend to be favoured. In the US, breeders recognize four different groupings, based on the weight of adult dogs. The Maxi is the largest, tipping the scales at over 19lb (9kg), while the Miniature, also known as the Mini, weighs in at 13 to 18lb (6-8kg). Toys weigh less than 12lb (5kg), and the smallest are sometimes described as Teacup Toys, weighing less than 6lb (2.5kg) when adult. (These are more popular in North America than elsewhere.) In the UK, most Cockapoos at present are mid-size, typically the result of crossings involving Miniature, rather than Toy, Poodles.

For these reasons, there is also a considerable difference in size between the heaviest and lightest of these dogs, which, in turn, influences all aspects of their lifestyle, ranging from the size of bed they will need through to feeding costs. Nevertheless, it may be worth exercising caution about acquiring a very small Toy Cockapoo, simply because miniaturization has tended to be accompanied by a loss of soundness as far as dog breeds are concerned – not least in the case of the Toy Poodle, which was bred down in size from the Miniature.

Choosing & buying

The first step will be to track down a breeder, which will be easier to do if you live in a country where there is a well-established breed organization. The US is such a country; you can find lists of breeders on the Cockapoo Club of America's website, for example, along with information on their health screening procedures and details about the current availability of puppies. Many of these breeders also have their own websites, where you can learn more about their dogs. A particularly important consideration to bear in mind is the likely size of the dog when adult, which will be determined primarily by that of its Poodle parent. Even with a reasonably large choice of breeders, however, you may still have to wait until a litter of puppies is available.

The adult size of a Cockapoo depends mainly on which type of Poodle contributed to its ancestry – Toy, Miniature or Standard.

Where no national organization exists, locating a breeder can be more difficult. The best way to start is probably via an internet search for the country in which you live, which should turn up breeders with their own websites. Such people are likely to be serious about their breeding programmes and keen to promote the Cockapoo, rather than simply breeding the dogs with little or no regard for their welfare. Once again, however, you may need to be patient and wait for puppies to become available.

You can search for advertisements in local newspapers or on the web, but this can be risky as a combination of relative scarcity of puppies and the Cockapoo's growing popularity has meant that some are seeking to exploit the situation financially. Be particularly careful under these circumstances that the puppies have not come from a puppy farm. If you decide to pursue this course, however, then the most critical thing will be to see both parents in home surroundings, which will also reassure you that you are actually purchasing a genuine Cockapoo, rather than some other crossbreed. You also need to be certain that breeding stock has been properly checked and certified for possible congenital illnesses (see page 16), and see the relevant paperwork. No responsible breeder will withhold this; if someone is reluctant to provide such information, continue your search for a puppy elsewhere.

When to buy

Domestic dogs have a limited breeding period, with bitches able to conceive only twice a year, and so the availability of puppies tends to be restricted. The ideal time to acquire a puppy is in the spring or early part of the summer, since this is the best time of year to spend training a young dog outdoors. Consider how this may fit in alongside your holiday plans, however, because it is definitely not recommended to obtain a puppy and then have to make alternative arrangements for its care within a few weeks because you are going away. Dogs are very much creatures of habit, and it is important to build a bond and establish a routine with your new pet from the outset.

Think twice about getting your puppy around the Christmas period either, because he or she can easily be overlooked during this busy time. On the other hand, if you plan to spend a quiet Christmas at home, this can actually be quite a good opportunity to settle a new puppy into your life.

Ideally, you should see the young puppies for the first time when they are about a month old, before they are ready to go to a new home. This gives you an opportunity to check that they are being reared in the home environment, rather than in an outdoor kennel. Young dogs reared indoors are likely to be friendlier, since they will have had much greater contact with people during the

early stage of their lives, which is very important. You may have to travel some distance to see a breeder; it can be helpful to see photographs or even video footage, but the best way of deciding which puppy, if any, in a litter appeals to you will be to arrange a convenient time to visit. It is quite normal for a breeder to request a small deposit if you then choose a puppy, before it is independent and ready to go to a new home.

Making a choice

It can be very difficult to choose one puppy from a litter, but there are factors that may influence your choice. For example, colouring may play a part. It could be that you have your heart set on a Cockapoo of a particular colour, or alternatively, when you see the litter, there may be a puppy with markings that particularly appeals to you. There again, a puppy's overall appearance may attract you, as may its behaviour.

In a litter of F1 puppies, bred from a Poodle-Cocker Spaniel cross, there may be puppies which bear a greater resemblance to one parent than the other, even at this early age. Coat type, too, can be variable within a litter, although puppy coats are generally less profuse than those of adults. However, as mentioned earlier, if you are looking at puppies from a Cockapoo bloodline, the likelihood is that they will be more standardized in appearance.

A family affair. A young apricot Cockapoo is shown here with its mother (left), its Miniature Poodle father, right, and another poodle.

One puppy or two?

You may be tempted to consider two puppies instead of one, but think very carefully about this beforehand. Bear in mind that owning a second puppy will have a marked impact on your budget; not just doubling the weekly food bill, but also adding to other ongoing costs such as veterinary fees and boarding kennels, for example. A single puppy should settle very well with you, but having two puppies of the same age can make the training process more difficult. If you ultimately decide that you want another Cockerpoo in due course, you can acquire one at a later stage and it should then settle well into your household alongside your established pet.

The variability in the appearance of Cockapoos, including coat type, is demonstrated clearly by these two individuals.

Cockapoos are naturally social dogs, and will happily play together.

The gender of the puppy

The gender of your puppy should also be considered, although there is no real evidence to suggest in the case of the breeds that have contributed to the Cockapoo's development that there is a significant difference in temperament between dogs and bitches. Males may, however, be slightly bigger when adult. If you hope to breed with your puppy in due course, then it will be better to acquire a female, simply because you can arrange

Differences in appearance between Cockapoo parents and offspring can also extend to coat texture. The mother (on the left) has a much smoother coat than her offspring.

for her to be mated by a stud dog. In the case of a male this will be harder to organize, since you will need to reach a breeding arrangement with the owner of a bitch in order to obtain some puppies.

Although there may be little variation in temperament between Cockapoo dogs and bitches, there are some behavioural differences to consider. A male Cockapoo may be more inclined to stray, particularly if there is a bitch on heat in the neighbourhood, while if you opt for a female, you must contend with her twice-yearly periods of heat (seasons). At this time, not only will she attract males, she will also want to mate.

There is also the possibility of further complications, such as not uncommon false pregnancies. These are caused by a hormonal disturbance, and will become apparent about eight weeks after a period of heat, when the bitch would normally have given birth if she had mated. She is likely to become particularly attached to one or more of her toys, regarding these as her puppies, and can become uncharacteristically aggressive, snapping at anyone who tries to take them away from her. Her mammary glands may even produce milk. False pregnancies can also be linked to cases of the womb infection known as pyometra, which may manifest itself by symptoms that include her drinking more than usual and going off her food. Pyometra can sometimes be life threatening, and rapid veterinary attention is required.

However, if you want a Cockapoo bitch simply as a pet, then arrange for your dog to be neutered once she reaches around six months of age, which

Cockapoos are quite confident dogs, as shown here when meeting another dog out for a walk.

They are not usually aggressive – just keen to say hello.

will preclude such problems. The operation – known as spaying – is more invasive than in a male dog, however, since it entails opening the abdominal cavity. Neutering a male dog – known as – castration, is a much simpler and less costly procedure, which may be something to bear in mind when you are choosing a puppy. Neutering a male Cockapoo has the effect of reducing its tendency to stray in search of a bitch – which can happen from the age of about six months – and prevents other signs of sexual behaviour.

A Cockapoo puppy will soon settle in a new home, and come to recognize its owner. It will also appreciate a reassuring cuddle.

Vaccinations and paperwork

When you pick up your puppy, be sure to obtain its vaccination certificate, which will confirm it has completed its first course of vaccinations, and will show the date and the signature of the vet as well as the stamp of the practice where it was given. Puppies are generally vaccinated against distemper, canine infectious hepatitis, leptospirosis and parvovirus. Depending on where you live and your travel plans, protection against rabies may also be legally required. Other vaccines, against kennel cough, for example, may be recommended later.

It is very important to check how frequently the young Cockapoo has been dewormed. Worms can infect puppies while they are still in the womb, and early treatment is required to kill the parasites before they become established. You will need

Purchasing a cockapoo puppy checklist

✓ Locate suitable breeders

✓ Arrange to visit by appointment

✓ Decide if you want to place a deposit on a puppy (obtain a receipt, if so)

✓ Arrange to collect the puppy once it is fully weaned

✓ Check the puppy over again at this stage, and pay the balance, assuming all is well

✓ Obtain a diet sheet detailing what the puppy is eating, so you can provide similar meals when you first take it home

✓ Ask for a signed vaccination certificate and deworming information at the time of collection

A note of caution!

Is she or isn't she ...?

The variation in the appearance of Cockapoos means there can be no absolute certainty that dogs in a rescue centre which resemble Cockapoos are actually descended from Cocker Spaniel-Poodle matings, unless their parents can be seen, too. They could simply be descended from crossings between other Spaniels and a Poodle, or indeed, be the result of other pairings that have produced puppies which appear to look like Cockapoos. Unless an individual's background is known with certainty, you cannot be sure of its ancestry without recourse to expensive genetic tests.

Cockapoo puppies are all generally very cute, but don't rush your choice. Bear in mind that, hopefully, your new pet will be part of your daily life for some time.

to obtain a further supply of deworming tablets for your puppy from your vet so that you can carry on this treatment yourself (approximately every three months).

Because, of course, the Cockapoo is not a recognized purebred dog, you won't receive records of the type provided for

pedigrees. If you are particularly interested, however, the breeder may give you the details of the Cocker Spaniel and Poodle which were mated to produce your puppy, including their formal kennel names, and also possibly a copy of their pedigree certificates if these are available. Ask to have a copy of the certification for screening of the parents, however, to keep with your puppy's records.

It is vital that your young Cockapoo is vaccinated against the major killer illnesses of dogs. Keep the certificate in a safe place for when it needs to be updated.

Checking the puppy's health

Like all young animals, puppies sleep more than adult dogs, so do not be surprised if some of the puppies appear sleepy when you go to see them. They should soon awaken, though, when picked up.

Check first on the underside of the body, towards the abdomen. If there is an obvious swelling in the midline, this is an indication of an umbilical hernia, which may need surgical correction in due course. A particularly pot-bellied appearance in young puppies can be indicative of intestinal worms. Inspect the hairs closely, too, for signs of lice; you may notice the tiny egg cases attaching to individual hairs. Fleas may also be present on young puppies (see page 76).

The ears of an older Cockapoo may also be cause for concern. This is a reflection of its spaniel ancestry, with

Arrange a visit to your vet soon after acquiring your puppy so that its state of health can be carefully checked.

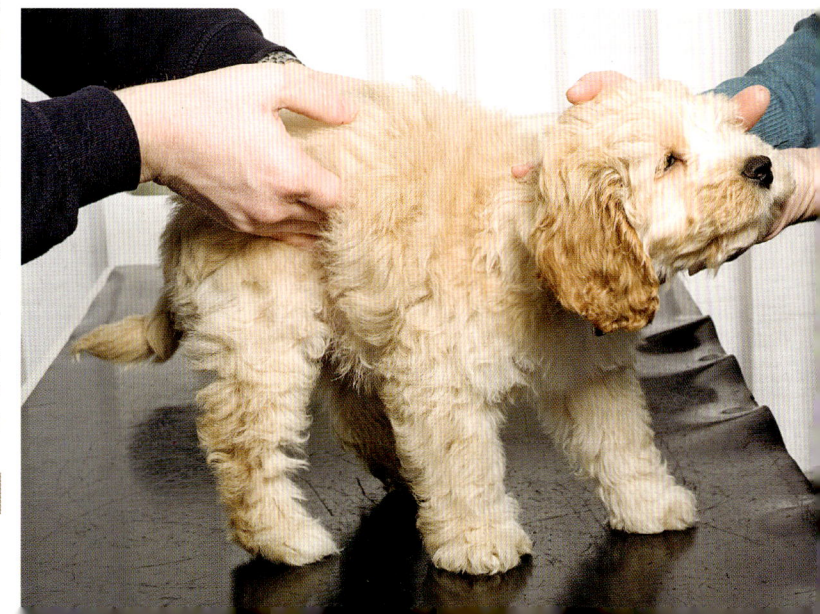

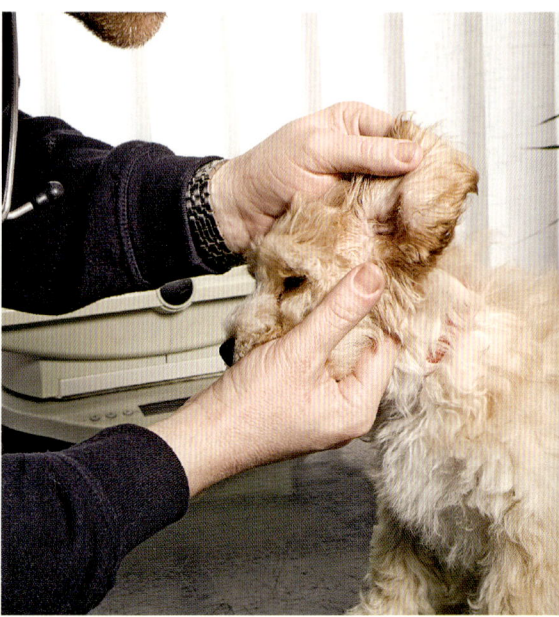

Above: Eye examinations on breeding stock are particularly significant, because they can eliminate inheritable ocular problems from Cockapoo bloodlines.

Above, right: Although the Cockapoo's ears are not as long and heavy as those of its Spaniel ancestor, the dogs can still suffer from similar ear infections.

dogs of this type being prone to ear infections because of the profuse covering of hair here, combined with the weight of the ear which restricts air flow. Repeated scratching is the most common sign of a problem, so lift the earflap and look for any blackish-brown waxy deposits within the entrance to the ear canal. This, at the very least, is likely to indicate dirty if not infected ears. Treatment of any infection here will require veterinary assistance.

Choosing an older Cockapoo

Most people are almost instinctively drawn to a puppy, but occasionally older Cockapoos find themselves in need of good homes. This can be for a variety of reasons, and such dogs are often handed over into the care of rescue centres. It's important to try and find out as much as possible about the background of a Cockapoo in these circumstances: it may simply be that its previous owner has fallen ill and is no longer able to look after their pet, or has even died; alternatively, the dog may have a behavioural problem which has resulted in the need for rehoming.

If you are interested in taking on a Cockapoo from a rescue centre, be as sure as you can that it will be compatible with your lifestyle. Bear in mind that it's impossible to age such dogs with any great certainty, especially once they enter middle age, so the animal may be older than you think. There is also, of course, the fact that you will probably be taking on an individual whose

Older Cockapoos can settle well in a new home, being quite adaptable by nature, but you will need to spend plenty of time with your new companion in order to build a bond between you.

It's not a good idea to change the name of an older Cockapoo when you acquire it, as doing so may mean that it will take longer to respond to you.

background is essentially unknown, which, of course, involves a risk that it might be affected by inherited conditions such as PRA (see page 16).

Whatever the circumstances, most rescue centres go to great lengths to ensure that their dogs pass into the care of considerate ownersm and are likely to want to visit your home to be sure that you can offer the Cockapoo a permanent, loving environment. They may also provide support if the dog is known to have any behavioural or chronic veterinary problems. In the case of a mistreated individual, however, this will call for particular understanding on your part; at the very least, you will need to be patient in order to win your pet's confidence. Always speak in a relatively quiet manner, and observe your pet closely. There can be seemingly innocuous things – even a coat of a particular colour – that may cause a rescued dog to display distinct signs of nervousness, presumably because it provides an unhappy reminder of its past.

Responsible rescue organizations are very wary about allowing any dog that has been abused to go to a home where there are younger children, especially if it has not lived in such a household previously. A puppy is likely to be a much more suitable choice where there are young children in the house, as it is more ready to fit in around them than will be an older dog.

Pet insurance

It is very important to be adequately insured when you acquire a dog, not just because of accidental damage that may pccur around the home (especially with a young Cockapoo), but also because of your legal liabilities. If your dog strays and causes an accident, you could end up facing a massive claim from the driver and any passengers in the vehicle if they have sustained injury. Third party cover is essential, therefore, because dog owners can be held legally liable under these circumstances. The policy should also provide you with the services of a lawyer if your dog is alleged to have bitten someone. Check your home insurance policy, as this may already include such cover. Another possibility is

Obtaining an older Cockapoo checklist

✓ Contact rescue centres
✓ Arrange to visit by appointment
✓ Interact with the dog, as permitted by the staff
✓ Be prepared to have a home visit
✓ Pick up your Cockapoo, along with vaccination certificate, and pay a rehoming fee
✓ Keep in touch, alerting the centre to any problems you encounter

that it may be incorporated in a policy alongside health care cover for your new pet, although if you are concerned, contact either your insurer or an insurance broker for advice.

Pet insurance cover will protect you from unexpected veterinary bills – should your dog be injured in an accident, for example – but does not cover routine costs such as vaccinations. As always, shop around to obtain the best cover for your needs, checking exclusions carefully. Pet insurance has become increasingly competitive over recent years, and the number of available policies has grown rapidly, too, so there are now more options to investigate. You may have more difficulty trying to insure an adult Cockapoo of unknown age, although dog rescue charities can sometimes help since they offer insurance policies themselves.

Preparing for your new pet

It is important to prepare your home for your new pet in advance. Ensure that the garden is adequately fenced, bearing in mind that dogs can be adept at finding an escape route. If it does get out, it is likely to be in great danger from road traffic. Check there are no gaps under fence panels through which a young Cockapoo could slip, and be sure that the posts here are firm as well. Bear in mind that adult dogs can also jump over barriers on occasions, so the fencing should therefore be tall enough to prevent your pet doing this. If you need to replace an area of fencing, it's usually better to erect a wooden fence rather than using wire mesh.

You may want to restrict

If your garden is not fully secure, you will need to go with your pet when it goes out to be sure it doesn't stray. You can also teach it to walk on the lead here.

the area where your Cockapoo can roam in the home, and a stairgate, often fitted to prevent toddlers climbing the stairs, is recommended to prevent access to upstairs rooms. There will also be times when you need to confine your puppy safely, and purchasing a crate for this purpose is recommended. Later, this can be used as a travelling container in the back of a hatchback or estate car (station wagon) when you go out with your dog. It ensures that the animal will not jump about within the vehicle, which could distract you and lead to an accident, and also prevents it from being thrown about inside the car should you brake or swerve suddenly. The other option is to obtain a dog guard designed to fit in the back of your particular car, or to use a special dog harness that attaches to the seatbelt which will achieve the same result.

While your new dog is still a puppy, it's quite likely that furniture and furnishings within the home may suffer damage caused by chewing. This can largely be avoided by providing chews to offset the pain of teething, although it may be worth temporarily rearranging the furniture so that any particularly cherished items are kept out of your dog's reach. Make sure, too, that there are no loose edges of carpet, which puppies often like to chew. Should there be a significant risk of this, you could consider purchasing cheaper rugs to cover the area until the chewing phase is over.

A sleeping and travelling pen suitable for a Cockapoo. Be sure to choose a size that is big enough for when your dog is fully grown.

If you have open fires, ensure these are properly screened to keep your puppy away from the hearth. Trailing electrical cables can be another serious danger when puppies are around, particularly if these extend to power points hidden in the room – behind a chair, perhaps. Here, a puppy may lay and gnaw at the cabling, with potentially fatal consequences. Keep cables off the floor as far as possible and, in areas of the home where your puppy can roam, always ensure they are disconnected from the power supply when not in use. The

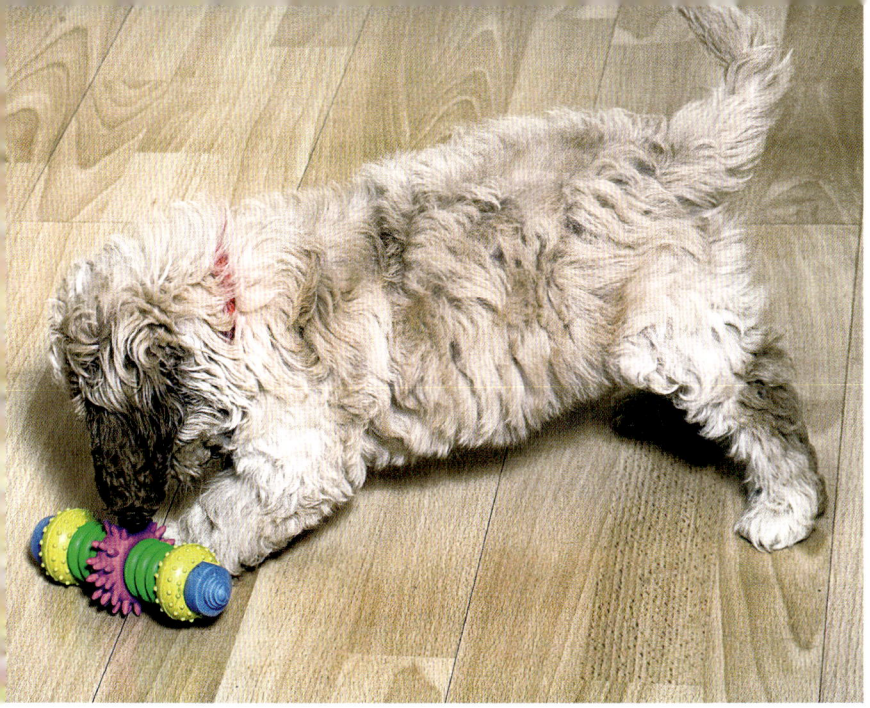

A range of toys will not only help to occupy your puppy, reducing the likelihood of it becoming bored and destructive, but should also serve to ease the pain of teething.

risk of electrocution is reduced with older Cockapoos, since they are less destructive, but they may still sweep lights off tables if they become entangled with the cabling.

Food for your Cockapoo

It is important to ascertain the type of food that your Cockapoo has been eating so that you can obtain a supply before collecting your puppy when it is about eight weeks old and fully weaned. Even if you want to change your dog's diet in due course, avoid doing so at first, because this is the stage when puppies are vulnerable to digestive upsets. Wait for a couple of weeks and then make changes gradually, over the course of a week or so, to allow the puppy's digestive system to adjust accordingly. This can be achieved easily by increasing the quantity of the new food offered at each meal while simultaneously reducing the amount of the original food.

You will also need both food and water bowls. These should be heavyweight or well balanced so that they cannot be tipped over, and it's also vital to be able to clean them easily. Most pet stores stock a good range, but try to choose bowls with relatively small diameters, otherwise the potentially long ears of the Cockapoo can become soiled by food or saturated with water whenever the dog eats or drinks. Earthenware is the traditional material used for bowls, but stainless steel and plastic containers are also available. Plastic is perhaps the least satisfactory option, since the puppy can easily gnaw this.

Above: Plastic food and water bowls are very stable, and can be easily cleaned, but beware that your puppy does not start to chew them.

Above, right: Puppies, and older dogs, too, will appreciate having a snug blanket where they can curl up to sleep. Place the bed in a quiet, draught-free part of your home.

Sleeping arrangements

It is generally not worth purchasing a bed for a puppy initially, because this is likely to be destroyed while the dog is teething, and, of course, a young dog will need a bigger bed as it grows. Much better to wait until the chewing phase has passed, and in the meanwhile, obtain a cardboard box of suitable dimensions, line the inside with soft bedding, and cut down one of the sides if necessary to allow your Cockapoo easy access into and out of the box. When the youngster gnaws the box, it can be easily replaced.

For an older Cockapoo, you can choose either a conventional plastic bed that can be lined with bedding, or a bed made from softer material that will allow your dog to stretch out comfortably. A beanbag is another option, as is a single duvet folded in half and covered with an easily made slipcase. Try to avoid beds with intricate designs, since these can be harder to clean properly, which is particularly important, not just to address the distinctive 'doggy odour' that can build up over time, but also in case you find fleas on your pet. Washing your pet's bedding will play an important part in eliminating these parasites, so be sure, too, that any covers can be removed for this purpose.

Bringing home your new pet

Try to arrange it so that you can do this in the earlier part of the day. Bear in mind that a young puppy will not have been in a vehicle before, so it may find the unfamiliar sensations of the journey rather distressing. There is even a risk that it could be carsick, particularly on a longer trip, so it's a good idea to confine the puppy in a suitable, ventilated carrier, available from pet shops and some veterinary surgeries, keeping the young dog in dimly lit surroundings for the duration of the journey. Line the carrier with clean newspaper and soft bedding, and place this on the floor behind the driver's or passenger's seat, where it is less likely to be exposed to direct sunlight than it would be in the back of a hatchback or on a seat.

With an older Cockapoo, it can help to have someone with you on the journey home, particularly if you do not have a dog guard in your car. Cover the back seat with a blanket, and persuade the dog to sit here with your travelling companion. Fit the dog into a canine safety harness (available from most pet stores) and connect this to one of the rear seatbelts as recommended by the manufacturer. This will also prevent the dog from attempting to jump about in the vehicle. Try to ensure the dog has a good walk before setting off, however, particularly if you have a long journey ahead of you and are not able to make

many 'comfort breaks.' After a walk, your new dog will also be less energetic and more inclined to settle down and sleep during the journey.

The way that you manage things when you get home will also have a direct influence on how your puppy settles in its new environment.

Your Cockapoo will want to explore its new surroundings before it goes to sleep. Keep a close eye on the puppy when it is investigating, however, to be sure it does not endanger itself.

Although not particularly elegant when running, Cockapoos can race around at a surprising pace, and display good stamina, too. Be careful not to over-exercise a young puppy, however.

An advantage of getting your puppy reasonably early in the day is that it can explore its environment and then, hopefully, will sleep well overnight. If you get home late, it is more likely to feel disorientated and will then be more reluctant to settle down, which is likely to apply in the case of an older dog, too.

Settling in

Although getting a Cockapoo will be an exciting event for you, the move is likely to be distressing initially for your dog, and particularly so for a puppy: this will probably be the first time that your new pet has been apart from the rest of its family.

Sleeping arrangements

Although most dogs adjust very quickly under these circumstances, the puppy may be reluctant to settle at night to begin with, or it might wake up and start howling. It may seem harsh, but

Provide your puppy with a bed where it will be able to sleep. Playing with it just before you go to bed is likely to make your young Cockapoo sleepy, too.

Support your puppy carefully when you pick it up, as shown here. Always hold the hindquarters, and remember, if it wriggles, that the claws can be sharp.

A hot water bottle filled with warm – not boiling – water, and carefully enclosed in a secure cover, can help to make up for the warmth of the littermates that your Cockapoo puppy will be missing at first.

the best thing is to ignore this; if you get up and try to comfort the puppy this will encourage similar behaviour in the future, and it will simply continue to do howl because it knows that it can get your attention this way. Equally, it is not a good idea to allow the young Cockapoo to sleep in your bedroom, because it will almost certainly have an accident here at some stage. It will also be much harder to persuade the Cockapoo to sleep elsewhere in the home once it is older.

House rules

Dogs are creatures of habit, and it is important to establish a routine to help them settle into their new home. Mealtimes and walks should be taken at set

Settling an older dog

An older dog is likely to settle down more readily at night, but you should begin to develop a routine right from the outset to facilitate this. First, take your Cockapoo out into the garden so it can relieve itself, or, better still, go for a walk. Place your new companion's bed in a quiet, draught-free part of the home, where it will remain relatively warm overnight, and it should settle down to sleep quite quickly. Keep the curtains drawn, since your dog may be more inclined to sleep in darkened surroundings and will not wake up so early in the summer.

times as far as possible. Dogs, and puppies in particular, also need periods of rest, and should be allowed sleep intervals during the day. This is especially worth bearing in mind if you have young children, who are likely to want to play with their new pet for long periods at first.

A puppy will probably want to relieve itself as soon as it wakes up, so take it to an area of the garden that you have chosen for this purpose. As soon as the young Cockapoo acts as required, praise it lavishly. Your tone of voice is important when training a dog; use an enthusiastic tone to reinforce correct behaviour, and adopt a firm or harder tone to register your displeasure if your dog behaves incorrectly.

Consistency is also a very important factor when settling your dog into the home. For example, if you do not want your Cockapoo to sit on your chairs

When you acquire an older Cockapoo, bring your new pet's bed home, too, even if you decide to replace it later, as it will help it settle.

Cockapoos are all individuals, and each will have its favourite playthings, including toys. To protect your pet from possible injury, it's important that toys meet appropriate safety standards.

Always encourage your puppy to relieve itself in the garden, developing a routine particularly first thing in the morning and again at night.

or sofa, don't encourage your dog to join you when you are sitting on the furniture, and then scold the animal if it jumps up later of its own accord. Should you acquire an older Cockapoo that has been allowed to sit on furniture in the past, it may be very difficult to break this behaviour pattern. The simplest option here may be to cover the furniture with a throw to provide protection. Most Cockapoos tend not to shed their coats, thanks to their poodle ancestry, but some individuals are more likely to lose hairs than others – especially if they are the result of an F1 cross reflecting a more dominant Spaniel influence.

Special pet vacuum cleaners are available for removing unwanted pet hairs from furniture and carpets. However, it is the dander (dandruff-like matter) that is more likely to generate an allergic response.

Other pets

You may already have other pets – possibly even another dog – that your Cockapoo must learn to live harmoniously alongside. When confronted with a

If you decide that you do not want your Cockapoo to sit on furniture, do not encourage your pet to jump on to chairs as a puppy, because it will then be much harder to dissuade the dog from doing so when it is older.

Warning signs

Keep a close watch on your puppy at first, and be aware of any problems that may arise due to its change of environment. Be alert particularly to any signs of diarrhoea. This is a serious condition in young dogs, particularly puppies, since they can rapidly become dehydrated with this ailment. Seek veterinary advice without delay if your Cockapoo puppy has diarrhoea, especially if there are any signs of blood. Older dogs, whose immune systems may be better developed, are less likely to fall ill following a move to a new home, although if this does happen, veterinary assistance will again need to be sought without delay. Offering the same food that your puppy has been eating will greatly reduce the likelihood of a problem of this type occurring.

cat, a puppy's natural reaction is usually to run enthusiastically up to the animal, which may then rush off or jump onto a surface out of reach. If this happens, a firm "No" will help the puppy to associate both the word and your tone of voice with this unwanted behaviour on its part. If cornered, your cat may seek to reinforce the 'no chasing' message in its own way by lashing out with its claws. This is definitely not to be recommended or encouraged, because sharp claws can easily scratch the puppy's eyes. It will not be long before your puppy learns to leave its feline housemate alone, and domestic harmony is restored. A badly trained dog is a liability to itself, its owners, and everyone else, and a puppy must be taught correctly at the outset what is acceptable behaviour and what is not.

Equally, you should also try and keep a Cockapoo away from small pets such as rabbits, which will be less able to defend themselves. If you have a hamster, pet bird, or other small animal that you want to let out of its cage from time to time, be sure the puppy is excluded from the room when this happens.

When it comes to encouraging a new puppy to bond with an existing dog in your household, there are steps that you must take to ensure they will start living together in relative harmony right from the outset. Flashpoints are most likely to arise at mealtimes, and the dogs should be fed separately, even in different rooms if necessary, so there's be no risk of one being able to steal the other's food.

When meeting for the first time, do not force the dogs together, but instead allow them to get to know each other on their own terms while you watch discretely nearby. Your established pet is likely to sniff at the puppy, and perhaps follow it if it tries to walk away. Do not intervene or try to reassure the puppy

at this stage, since this will be counterproductive in allowing the dogs to form a relationship together, and establish their appropriate hierarchical positions within the family 'pack.' The best course of action is simply to reinforce this natural hierarchy (in which the puppy is the underdog), by paying rather more attention to the existing dog than to the newcomer when they are together. Before long, you should find that domestic harmony prevails and your dogs are the best of friends.

It can be harder introducing an adult Cockapoo to a home with another dog, because your existing pet may be more territorial in this situation. Try to introduce the dogs on neutral ground, therefore, so they can become acquainted before bringing the newcomer home. Factors that are likely to influence the chances of success include the ancestry, age and gender of both dogs. Two intact males are least likely to accept each other, although neutered males will probably be far more amenable, whilst a male dog and a bitch are more likely to get on together than two males.

If you already have a dog, do not undermine its position or make it jealous by giving too much attention to the newcomer. Two young dogs like these are likely to accept each other more readily.

Food and feeding

Dogs are omnivorous in their feeding habits. Like their wild ancestor, the Grey Wolf (Canis lupus), dogs rely mainly on protein and fat – the key ingredients of meat – rather than on carbohydrate, which is not widely found in the wolf

Cockapoos are quite
adaptable, and will
play readily with
people and other
canine members of
the household.

diet. However, carbohydrate – derived from cereal crops – is found in most dog foods because it is a cheap way of providing energy.

Apart from these 'macronutrients,' dogs require in the diet a range of minerals as well as inorganic chemicals known as trace elements. The most important mineral is calcium, which is vital for a healthy skeletal system, as well as for the transmission of electrical impulses along the body's pathway of nerves. Trace elements are needed in smaller amounts for healthy functioning of the body, and include iodine, a key component utilized by the thyroid glands in the neck. They produce hormones that have widespread actions around the body, affecting its metabolism. Vitamins also play a series of diverse roles in the body, with dogs requiring thirteen different ones in total. Members of the Vitamin B complex are important in preventing deficiency diseases, while Vitamin D is linked with calcium metabolism. These chemicals must normally be present in the diet, since they cannot be manufactured in the body, although some dogs can make Vitamin C to protect them against contracting scurvy.

Types of prepared foods

Most modern dog foods are of the 'complete' type, consisting of a balanced ration that has been formulated to meet the known nutritional needs of dogs, and including all the necessary macronutrients along with essential minerals, trace elements and vitamins. These foods can be fed straight from the packet, with no further preparation or supplementation required.

Two basic types of complete food exist: 'wet' dog food is available in either cans or in plastic pouches, each of which usually contains a single meal; the second type of complete dog food is often known as dry food. Most dogs generally prefer wet food, although dry food offers a much more concentrated ration. Because dry food has less water, dogs fed on this type of food will drink more water as a consequence to maintain their fluid intake. Dry food can simply be stored in a cool, dry place, out of direct sunlight – unlike a can of dog food, which should be kept in a refrigerator once opened. Some dog owners prefer to give their pets prepared meat from a tin. This is usually served with a portion of dried biscuit-type food called 'mixer' that also contains various essential supplements. Feeding guidelines are provided on the packaging of both tinned meat and mixer.

Make sure you store all foods in a cool, dry place. Mixer-type foods benefit from being kept in airtight containers so they keep fresh and don't attract rodents. Any unused meat from a can should be transferred to a closed plastic container and placed in the fridge until needed for the next meal.

Do not alter the young Cockapoo's diet immediately after you acquire your new pet. Any changes should be made gradually, over a week or so. Remember, too, that dry food is a concentrated ration, so don't exceed the recommended feeding quantities.

Special diets

There are now a number of foods available, in both wet and dry ranges, catering for dogs at different stages of their lives. For example, these include puppy foods, which are usually recommended up to the age of six months of age, as well as foods for dogs described as 'seniors,' which are typically over seven years old. These diets are adjusted slightly, in terms of their nutritional values, to meet the specific needs of dogs in each of the age categories.

If you are unfortunate enough to have a Cockapoo that suffers from a food allergy, your vet may recommend one of the so-called 'hypoallergenic' diets, typically based around meat such as venison, which may not trigger your dog's sensitivity. It is also possible to obtain vegetarian diets for dogs, which are again supplemented with all the necessary ingredients required to keep your pet in good health. Unlike cats, dogs are not obligate carnivores, and so can be fed this sort of diet, although some owners complain that such foods will trigger more severe flatulence in their pets than meat-based foods, particularly when they are first fed these foods.

Feeding guidelines

Whichever type of food you are using, be sure to read the information on the packaging, because feeding instructions – particularly relating to the quantities that should be offered – can differ quite significantly. Also bear in mind the likely weight of your dog, since this has a direct influence on the amount of food it requires. A potentially small Cockapoo bred from a Toy Poodle ancestor will obviously need less food than one created from a Standard Poodle parent.

The shelf-life of both wet and dry dog food may extend over many months, and often for a year or more. However, if you obtain a large sack of dry food, it will need to be used once it is opened, and storage can be a problem. Luckily, dogs are far less fussy about their food than cats, and so they are unlikely to refuse to eat a particular brand once you are halfway through a sack. Purchasing a large sack is likely to be the most cost-effective way of feeding your pet. However, consider, from your dog's point of view, whether this type of food will be as appetising and interesting as some others ...

Early training

You should begin basic training as soon as you obtain your puppy, well before it will be ready to go outside into a park for a walk. The most important simple commands to teach at this stage are "Come" and "Sit," and both of these can be linked to mealtimes to reinforce the message. Cockapoos are generally keen to learn, with repetition playing an important role in reinforcing the training.

One of your first decisions is to choose a name for your puppy. The actual name is really not as significant as the sound, but to prevent possible confusion in the young dog's mind it is better to avoid using one that is close to the sound of another family member's name. Always use its name when training your Cockapoo, so that the puppy comes to recognize the sound.

Training at mealtimes

A puppy will soon settle into the routine of its new home, and will be eager for its meals. So, having tipped the required amount of food into its bowl, call the puppy to you, using the instruction "Come," followed by its name. The puppy will learn very quickly to associate this sound with food, and will come running to you. Always praise the puppy in an enthusiastic voice when it does this, to reinforce the message. Then, before you place the food bowl on the ground, ask the young dog to "Sit." In its excitement, however, the puppy is unlikely to respond as required, particularly at first. Do not tease the young Cockapoo if it fails to comply with your instruction by taking the food away, as this will just make it anxious, nervous, and potentially aggressive about food. Instead, gently put your hand over your puppy's hindquarters, and exert a little pressure here, which should result in the dog sitting down. Praise your pet again at this stage, before placing the food bowl on the ground.

Going through these stages before every meal will soon result in your puppy learning both how to come and also how to sit when instructed. (You can also introduce these instructions at other times – when you are going out into the garden to play, for example – and this will provide further reinforcement of what is required.) After it has eaten, a young puppy will want to relieve itself, so you should place it outside immediately. It helps if you have selected an area of the garden where it will be relatively easy to clear up and clean after your pet has finished.

Train your puppy to sit, rather than leap around excitedly, when you put the food bowl on the floor.

Bitches, in particular, should not be encouraged to urinate randomly over a lawn, because the acidity of their urine can cause the grass to form bare patches.

An older Cockapoo

Hopefully, an older Cockapoo will have already mastered such basics as coming when called before you acquire it, but you may encounter a problem if you decide to alter your dog's name, which is likely to confuse it. Thus, if the dog is already well trained, try to avoid changing its name unless this is really essential. Dogs can learn new names, but may set back training in other areas. You can still run through the same basic training with an adult Cockapoo as with a puppy. Since these dogs are intelligent and keen to learn, they will soon pick up what is required, even if they have not been well trained in the past. Help is also available at dog training classes, and if you encounter a particular problem it should be possible to book an individual session with a trainer with a view to overcoming it.

Choosing a vet

A number of different factors may affect your choice of veterinary practice. If you have had a dog before, or have other pets, you may already be using a practice where you can take your Cockapoo. Alternatively, you can ask

pet-owning friends and colleagues in your area for recommendations, or simply use the phone book and pick several practices near you at random. Call them and ask about the costs of vaccination and neutering – the major veterinary expenses that you are likely to face during the first year of owning a Cockapoo. Proximity to the practice can be important, however, particularly if you are faced with an emergency at any stage. You may also want to ascertain whether you are likely to see the same vet on each visit. This can be helpful if your dog needs an ongoing course of treatment. Also, if time is an issue, you may prefer a practice which operates on an appointments system, rather than simply turning up with your dog and finding a large queue of people and pets in the waiting room.

Hand signals, as well as your tone of voice, are important when training your Cockapoo. If you acquire an older Cockapoo, it may already have had some training.

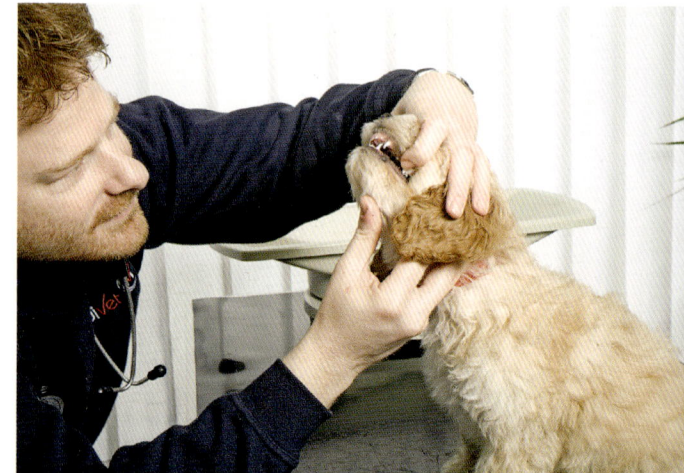

Above: It is important that puppies do not become distressed by a visit to the vet, because this can make trips here more difficult as your dog grows older.

Above, right: A thorough examination will include looking at the puppy's teeth and mouth. Continue to encourage your puppy to allow you to open its mouth regularly, since this will be useful in the future – for example, when brushing its teeth or giving tablets.

Right: A careful inspection of the ears can reveal the presence of mites that will need to be treated. Always suspect an ear problem if your Cockapoo begins to scratch its ears more than usual.

It is essential that your Cockapoo be checked over by a vet as soon as possible after you get it. A thorough check will include a cardiac examination, for example, and if an anomaly shows up you can raise the matter with the breeder straight away and decide what to do next – possibly even returning the puppy to the breeder in a worst-case scenario.

Microchipping

A visit to the vet at this time also provides the opportunity to arrange for your new pet to be microchipped. This process does not supplant the need for your dog to wear an identity medallion or tag on its collar, but does mean that the animal can still be identified if the medallion is lost for any reason. The microchip carries a unique number that is stored on a central database set against your name and contact details. Any stray dogs brought into rescue organizations are routinely checked for the presence of a microchip, and this process can reunite a Cockapoo with its owner.

The microchip, about the size of a grain of rice, is simply implanted under the skin at the back of the neck using a tool rather like a syringe. It should stay in position here, and will only be read when a special scanner is passed over this area, transmitting the microchip's unique numerical code. The sealed microchip has no power source and is inert, lasting throughout the dog's life.

Below, left: A microchip will provide a lasting means of identification, and is located in the dog's neck. The insertion procedure is essentially painless.

Below: Passing the reader over the microchip activates it, transferring the code back to the machine so that it can be read.

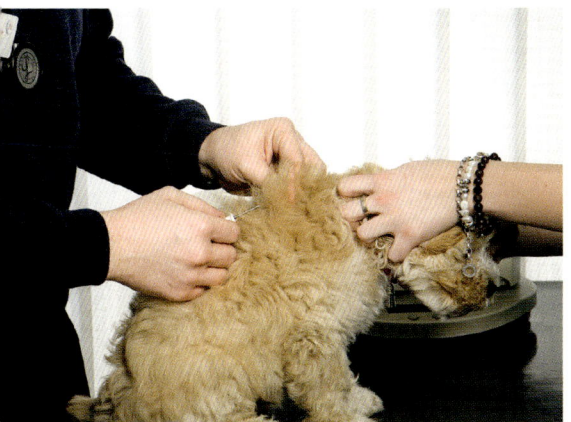
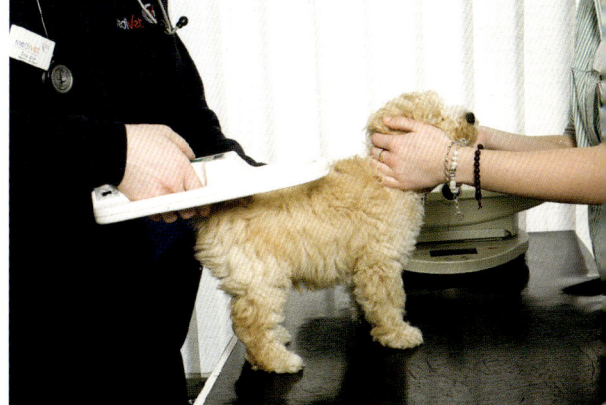

Vaccinations

It is very important to obtain the Cockapoo's vaccination certificate when you pick up your pet. This tells your vet when the animal was last vaccinated and what type of protection it has received. Puppies are usually given their first vaccines at about eight weeks of age, followed by a second set a month later. Thereafter, immunity is maintained by administering annual boosters.

You cannot safely take a puppy into public areas until several weeks after it has completed its initial vaccinations, because before that time it won't have developed full immunity. Therefore, when visiting the vet during this period, you should consider carrying the young dog as a precautionary measure, particularly if it was given no protection by its previous owner. Even after initial vaccinations have been completed, it is important that immunity is kept up to date by ensuring your dog receives the necessary booster doses at the recommended intervals. All the diseases that are vaccinated against – distemper, infectious canine hepatitis, parvovirus and leptospirosis – are potential killers, and even if a dog survives the initial infection there are likely to be lifelong adverse effects on its health. It simply is not worth taking the risk of leaving your pet unvaccinated.

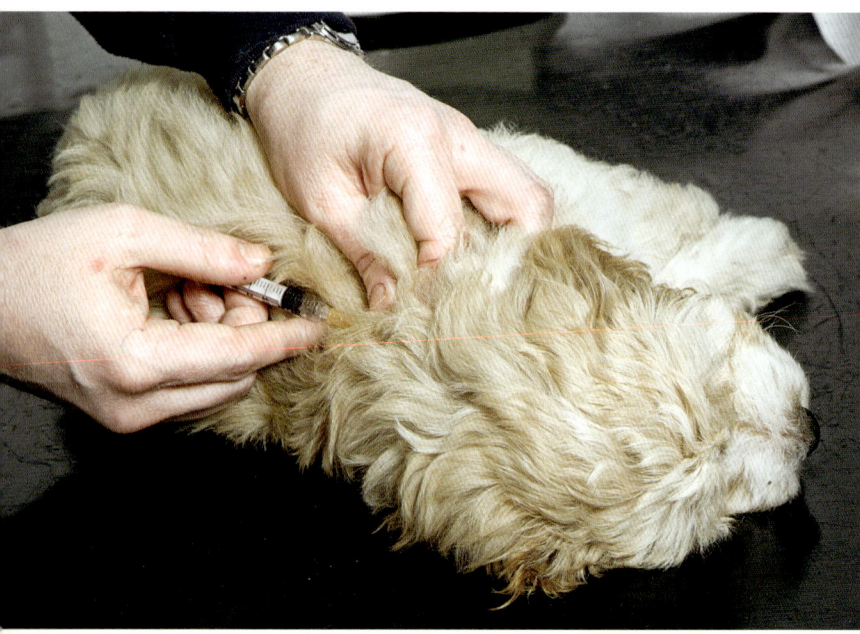

Vaccinations are generally given through the loose skin (scruff) at the back of the neck, and will usually cause the puppy little discomfort.

Vaccination will also be essential if you go on holiday. All reputable kennels will insist on seeing a vaccination certificate, and additional protection against kennel cough may also be recommended. This infection spreads easily in boarding kennels, and although the vaccine does not guarantee to protect your dog against all the infectious agents responsible for this illness, it does protect against the majority. The kennel cough vaccine offers relatively short-term immunity, however, and is simply squirted up the dog's nasal passages, rather than being injected under the skin, as with other vaccinations.

Rabies

This is a particularly serious viral disease, firstly because it is fatal in dogs, but also because it can be transmitted via the dog's saliva into the human body through a cut or bite. Rabies in people is often fatal, too, and the infection is prevalent in many parts of the world, only absent from islands such as Australia, Iceland, Cyprus, and the British Isles. There is now a vaccine to protect dogs against rabies, and its use is compulsory in some areas. Furthermore, only dogs protected by a rabies vaccination are allowed to travel under the UK's Pet Passport Scheme. However, since the infection is not present in the UK, dogs are not routinely vaccinated against it there.

Deworming

Your vet will also be able to advise you regarding deworming your puppy, and can provide suitable medication for this purpose. This is particularly important, because young puppies often acquire roundworms from their mother while they are developing in her body. Repeated early treatment should, however, eliminate the worms before they can start multiplying (the eggs are expelled from the body in the dog's faeces). Once the egg-laying stage is reached, screening from a faecal sample can help to identify dogs which are infected.

Humans can also accidentally ingest the microscopic roundworm eggs, and, if swallowed, these may hatch in the intestine. The immature worms then enter the bloodstream in a phase known as 'visceral larval migrans.' On rare occasions they can migrate to the eye, causing blindness. Children are particularly at risk when playing with a puppy because they frequently put their fingers in their mouths. Also, they may not always wash their hands before picking up food. Cleanliness is therefore very important as a way of safeguarding against picking up a roundworm infection.

It is usual to dose puppies every two to three weeks up to the age of three months. The tablets for the treatment can be easily administered, either disguised in food or given directly. To give them directly, have someone hold the puppy's hindquarters, place your left-hand thumb and fingers either side of the upper jaw (assuming you are right-handed), and tilt the dog's head back. Pick up the deworming tablet in your other hand and, using the index finger, gently push down the lower jaw and carefully drop the tablet as far back into the mouth as possible. Keeping the head upright, close the jaws again, and stroke the dog's throat, which should encourage your Cockapoo to swallow the tablet.

Treatment against tapeworms may also be required. These parasites can be picked up from fleas. Also, if you live in an area where heartworms and/or hookworms are present, talk to your vet about medication for your pet at the outset.

Establishing a routine

As already mentioned, dogs are creatures of habit, and it's a good idea to establish a daily routine for your Cockapoo as soon as possible. This will also simplify house-training; indeed, your first job each morning should be to put your puppy in the garden and encourage it to relieve itself. Once it has finished, call the young dog back inside and praise it when it comes with you.

The next part of your routine will probably be to feed the young Cockapoo. When the food is ready, encourage the puppy to sit, rather than running around excitedly as you are about to put the food bowl down on the floor. A healthy puppy is likely to eat its food rapidly. After it has eaten, if the weather is fine, take your puppy back out into the garden for a while, so that it can explore there under supervision. Before long, however, it is likely to want to sleep: your puppy will soon recognize its own bed and curl up there, but initially you may need to put the young dog in its bed, stroke it and talk gently to it to encourage it to settle down.

This is a good time to get your Cockapoo familiar with a crate, so that it does not resent being confined there if it is tired. Using a crate will make life safer for your puppy while it is very young: it cannot slip out of a door unnoticed,

Puppies of both sexes will urinate at first by squatting, and only when males are approaching sexual maturity will they raise their legs for this purpose (and some females will do this also on occasion).

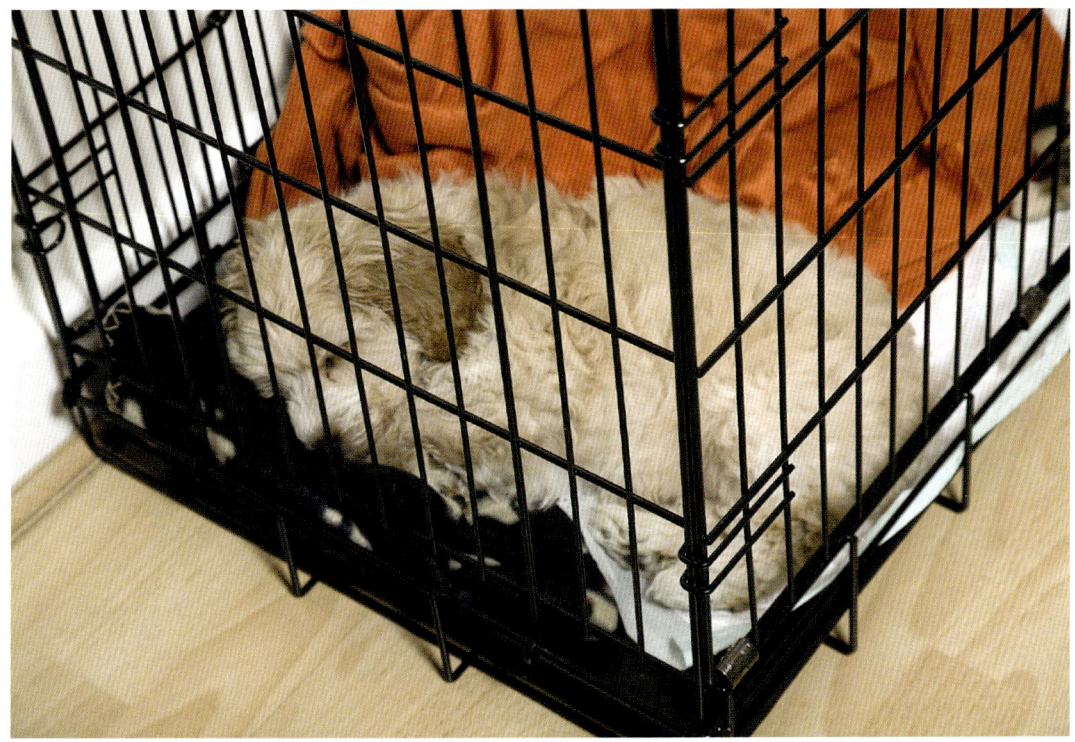

or end up injuring itself around the home. You can also be certain that your young Cockapoo won't be in any danger when you go out.

The senses and communication

Dogs perceive the world differently from humans, and rely on a combination of their senses. Cockapoos have a keen sense of vision and acute hearing, and their relatively broad nostrils give them a good sense of smell, as well. They can see in colour, although not as well as we can, but their vision is superior to ours at night, since they are able to see under conditions which would appear as total darkness to our eyes.

A Cockapoo has a reflective layer on the retina at the back of each eye, known as the tapetum lucidum, which helps to reflect available light and make images clearer, especially at night. Cockapoos also possess binocular vision, like other dogs. Because they receive overlapping images from both eyes, they can pinpoint the position of objects in front of them with great accuracy. This means, for example, that they can focus on, and pick up, a moving ball with ease.

A young Cockapoo puppy asleep in its pen. A young dog will soon feel secure in these surroundings, retreating here for a snooze when it is tired.

Their hearing is also significantly better than ours. They can detect sounds at a much higher frequency – which will be evident if you use a special dog whistle. The sound from the whistle will be inaudible to your ears, but can be heard by your dog even if it is some distance away and has disappeared from sight in undergrowth. While we can detect sounds up to 20,000Hz, Cockapoos may be able to hear frequencies of up to 100,000Hz, which falls within the range of ultrasound. Nevertheless, just as our hearing range declines with age, so does that of the Cockapoo. In some cases, dogs may actually become deaf in old age, and their eyesight can fail, too, with whitish cataracts developing in their eyes.

A Cockapoo's olfactory ability will vary through its life. Young puppies have a very restricted sense of smell at first, but adult dogs can develop an acute sense of smell, some 100 times better than our own. If you look closely at the nostrils of the Cockapoo you will see that these are effectively mobile on their outer edges, which enables them to be flared. As a consequence, the dog can increase the volume of air that it inhales, triggering specialist scent detector cells lining the nasal cavity.

Dogs rely much more heavily on non-verbal communication to express their moods than many people think. Barking is the most obvious form of communication, the meaning varying according to tone. A deeper, determined bark is more indicative of aggressive intent than a frequent, short bark, which can mean either frustration or excitement. When you are training your Cockapoo, it is important to be aware of the signs of body language. An excited and enthusiastic dog will raise its tail and lift the position of the ears, giving its face an alert expression. If nervous or scolded, however, a Cockapoo will lower its tail and hold the ears back against the body in an attempt to look smaller and therefore less threatening.

The learning process

The Cockapoo's ancestors have instincts honed over generations, particularly as far as hunting and retrieving are concerned, and are easily trained. Cockapoos are also very responsive to training. A puppy, in particular, is likely to make a good pupil, because at this relatively young age it will be more receptive than an older dog as it learns about the world. There are certain things to bear in mind when training a Cockapoo, however – not least of which is the fact that these dogs have a capacity for independent thought! This, again, is probably a reflection of their ancestry, since they frequently needed to act spontaneously when working.

Some puppies will learn more rapidly than others, and may well master

Smell is a very important sense for all dogs, and scent provides them with a great deal of information about their environment – both inside the home and outside – which will not be apparent to us.

some commands more readily. This is quite normal, although there are certain steps to take which will help the training process. To begin with, choose a locality where your puppy can concentrate without any distractions. Keep training sessions short; puppies learn by repetition, and so repeating the same thing frequently in several sessions every day will be much more effective than having a marathon session once a week, as a young puppy will soon lose interest under these circumstances. Even if your puppy does not always respond as required, be patient. Positive reinforcement is by far the most effective way of teaching a puppy: by giving encouragement, your puppy will fairly soon learn what is expected.

House-training

Follow the feeding guide given to you by the puppy's breeder, spacing the requisite number of meals throughout the day. Always give your puppy an opportunity to go out into the garden before and after a meal. It will soon learn what is required, although some puppies do appear to pick things up quicker than others. Although accidents invariably happen around the home, puppies are generally clean by nature. Initially, however, they will not indicate when they need to go out, but placing your pet outside regularly throughout the day should mean there will be few, if any, accidents. You can get training devices, including puppy pads, which can be useful for when the puppy is in the crate, but in general the best and quickest way to house-train a puppy is to anticipate when it needs to go outside, and thereby pre-empt any accidents around the home. Should these happen, however, it is very important to clean up thoroughly afterwards with an appropriate cleaning agent, otherwise a puppy will be drawn back to use the same spot again by the lingering scent, even though this may actually be undetectable to our noses.

Clearly, disinfecting the area is important, but such products must be used carefully, not least because they may cause permanent damage to carpets. In addition, some will actually reinforce the scent rather than eliminate it – especially pine-based disinfectants. It is therefore best to buy one of the products specially developed for use in cleaning up after puppies. You can also buy a product that attracts the dog to an area outdoors that you have specifically chosen for it to use. However, the potency of such products will be rapidly diluted by rain, and the outside area will need to be treated again to draw your puppy's attention to it.

Obedience training

Always use your puppy's name when calling it, and try to ensure that the young

Puppy pads can help with house-training, encouraging the puppy to relieve itself in a particular locality, but the best solution is to start training your pet to go outside for this purpose as soon as possible.

Treats can be offered as rewards as part of the training process, but always use them very sparingly, and opt for healthy treats as far as possible.

Cockapoo receives a reward when it responds to you. This does not have to be food, though; in fact, it is not a good idea to rely heavily on treats as part of the training process: not only will this predispose your pet to obesity and potential associated health problems such as heart disease and diabetes mellitus, it also tends to distract from the training process if you give a treat every time, as the young dog comes to focus on being given the treat, rather than what it is supposed to be doing. Simply praising your pet, stroking it, or playing a game are all ways you can reward the puppy for coming when called without having to resort to food. As healthy treats you can use small pieces of chopped carrot from time to time – which have the added benefit of keeping the teeth clean – which dogs in general will eat readily.

It is very important to spend plenty of time with your Cockapoo, especially when it is growing up, and to encourage other members of the family to become involved in the training process, too. Both of the Cockapoo's ancestral breeds were developed to work closely with a handler in the field, but if all the family gets accustomed to being with the dog on a regular basis there should then be no risk of your Cockapoo becoming a 'one person dog' that does not relate well to other family members.

Walking on the lead

Although it won't be possible to take the young Cockapoo out into public places until it has completed its course of vaccinations, it is important to begin basic lead training before this time at home. Initially, the first step is to persuade your pet to wear a collar. Measure around the neck to ensure that the collar will fit, allowing space for an extra two fingers at the front so it is not tight. You will need to let the collar out as the puppy grows. You must also fit an engraved disc giving your address and a contact telephone number in case your Cockapoo strays, although the microchip (see page 55) offers a more permanent means of identification that cannot be lost. The choice of material for the collar and the accompanying lead is a matter of personal preference. Nylon items are tough and will be cheaper than leather ones, but will not feel as smooth. When you first fit the collar, do not be alarmed if your puppy tries to remove it. This is quite normal, and within a day or so, the young dog will have become used to it.

The next step is to attach the lead, but don't expect your puppy to react well to this either at first. It may even refuse to walk, preferring to roll over in an attempt to chew at the lead. Gently distract it from this behaviour, and once again your pet will soon accept being on the lead. Once you start walking with your puppy on the lead you are likely to be confronted by another problem: it will pull in all directions. Initially, therefore, walk the puppy alongside a wall or a fence

An extending lead can be very useful when taking a Cockapoo out for a walk, since it can be used to prevent the dog from pulling ahead or straying into the road.

— up your driveway, for example — while keeping the dog on your left-hand side. This means that the puppy can only go in a straight line, and you can concentrate on preventing it from pulling ahead, particularly if you keep the lead relatively taut at this stage.

It will take time for your puppy to learn what is required. Short training sessions, lasting five to ten minutes and repeated throughout the course of the day, will be far more effective than an occasional marathon lesson. Keeping your puppy's concentration is important, and training can be achieved much more effectively this way. Try to ensure there are no distractions, either, like

Attaching a lead to the collar of a young Cockapoo. It will probably take a few days for the puppy to become accustomed to wearing its collar.

At first, your puppy will resent being attached to a lead. It may well attempt to chew through it, as shown, so a tough nylon design is recommended.

It will usually only take a few days for a young dog to become used to its lead, and at this stage you can then begin to encourage it to walk alongside you, as the next part of the training process.

other members of the family in the garden at the same time. Integrate other aspects of the puppy's training into the walking routine, such as asking it to sit, because this is something that will be required on occasions when you are out together. It also prevents training from becoming too predictable, causing the puppy to lose interest.

There are other valuable lessons that you can begin to teach when the puppy is in the garden off its lead. Obviously, you can call it to come to you, but it's also a good opportunity to play ball. Both of the Cockapoo's ancestral breeds are retrievers, and so most Cockapoos will bring a ball back almost instinctively as part of a game. This then provides an opportunity to teach two further important lessons, one of which is to ask the puppy to drop the ball when instructed. This can prove very important later in the young dog's life if, for example, it has picked up something in its mouth that could be harmful.

A Cockapoo puppy will readily play with a ball, but make sure that the toy is large enough so that it cannot be accidentally swallowed.

Initially, of course, the puppy is unlikely to know what it is required to do, and you will have to take the ball gently out of its mouth. This then offers another opportunity for important training. Place your left hand over the puppy's upper jaw, assuming that you are right-handed, and lift the dog's head up slightly. Then, with your right hand, gently prise open the lower jaw, which will result in the ball falling on to the ground. Teaching your dog to let you open its mouth in this way can be very helpful should you need to give it a deworming tablet or some other medication. It can also enable you to brush its teeth, which should be done on a regular basis to help prevent a build-up of tartar on them. Tartar can lead to gum disease and cause the dog to lose some of its teeth in later life. Special canine toothbrushes and toothpaste that will not foam in the mouth are available, but you need your dog's cooperation in order to use them.

Venturing further afield

When your Cockapoo has completed its vaccinations it will be safe to take it outside into public places, so choose a suitable part of your neighbourhood to begin exercising the dog. To start with, this should be somewhere you are unlikely to encounter too many other dogs while you continue your puppy training, and you should certainly choose a location well away from farm animals as well. It is also important to introduce your Cockapoo to the sights and sounds of urban living, so that the dog becomes confident at walking on the lead near traffic, and becomes used to other new sounds. Therefore, quiet footpaths and side roads are a good place to start. Avoid busy junctions initially, because the noise and turbulence created by vehicles passing at close quarters will be unsettling for your pet. Do not forget to take some suitable bags with you to clear up if your pet defecates on the pavement. Follow the basic training routine that you have been pursuing at home, but do not be surprised if your Cockapoo is distracted and does not follow your instructions as diligently as it does at home.

For safety, ensure that you are positioned between your pet and the road when out walking.

When you come to a road junction, train your dog to always sit, until it is safe for you both to cross. With a young puppy, be sure that it cannot pull ahead into the road, by keeping a firm grip on the lead.

Continue with the same lead-training lessons you have already been doing, with the dog boxed in by a fence or wall for much of the time. Keep the Cockapoo walking on this side of the pavement; this should prevent it from straying into the path of other people coming towards you, or into the road. Until the puppy is adequately trained, safety in this situation depends partly on anticipation. Do not allow the young dog to pull ahead, and pause regularly, making it sit on the pavement from time to time. This is a lesson that will need to be reinforced whenever you come to a kerb before crossing the road.

Toys and treats

Successful training depends in part on building a bond between you and your pet, and play presents an important opportunity to create this bond. It also means that you will be able to teach your pet another important lesson – the need to drop items when instructed to do so.

The choice of toys for your Cockapoo is important. They should be robust, because if they can be destroyed easily there's a risk that parts may end up being swallowed, causing a serious blockage in your dog's digestive tract that can only be corrected by surgery. Provide only recognized brands of chew toys for your pet, therefore. A puppy's urge to chew will become most apparent when it is teething, just before six months of age. Toys that your Cockapoo can chase are also likely to be popular. They can be taught to catch flying discs, but you should only use the ones designed for dogs; children's toys of this type are unlikely to be sufficiently robust and are more liable to result in injury. Most Cockapoos prefer running after balls.

A wide range of different treats is available for dogs, but you should not be fooled into thinking that your puppy will be deprived if it doesn't receive a regular supply. There is actually no need to use treats at all, and if you rely on them too much for training purposes, a young Cockapoo will soon begin focusing on the treat rather than concentrating on the instruction. Treats can be used to maintain a dog's interest, though, and are most valuable in persuading your Cockapoo to return to you. They can be combined with clicker training – a method that employs a special device to make a clicking sound, letting the dog know that it has behaved as required. After a certain number of clicks, you can occasionally give a treat as well, reinforcing the positive message of the clicker.

There is certainly no need to use packaged treats for your pet. Small pieces of sliced carrot are a better alternative, since they will not add significantly to the dog's calorie intake. Prepared beforehand, they can be carried easily in your pocket in a plastic bag.

Different types of chews are available. Rawhide chews – as shown here – can safely be eaten by your dog. However, they can sometimes upset the digestive system, especially if eaten all at once.

Weight watching

Cockapoos can suffer from obesity and its complications if they are overfed, with treats adding unnecessarily to their calorie intake, especially if they are also not getting enough exercise. It is therefore important to keep a check on your dog's condition to ensure that it is not becoming overweight. This is

An assortment of the different toys available for dogs. There are toys that can be thrown for your dog to chase, others that can be used in a tug-of-war, and a third group that can be chewed.

This Cockapoo puppy is getting to grips with a pull or tug toy. Do not pull too hard when playing, since this might damage your dog's teeth. Just hold the toy firmly and let your pet pull, rather than trying to do so at the same time.

relatively unlikely in puppies, since they are so active, although one of the side-effects of neutering is often a gain in weight, due to changes in the dog's metabolism: to avoid this problem, cut back on the amount of food your Cockapoo is given after neutering. Obesity can dramatically shorten a dog's life, resulting in heart problems and the condition diabetes mellitus, as well as putting a strain on weight-bearing joints such as the hips and knees.

If you acquire a Cockapoo that is already overweight, check with your vet that there is no underlying medical condition that could be the cause of the problem. The practice will be able to work out an individual diet plan for your pet, which you should follow. This is likely to entail a reduction in the amount of food that you provide, and possibly also a switch to a so-called 'obesity diet' which has a relatively low nutrient, high fibre content. More exercise will also be important, too, to burn off the unwanted calories.

Grooming

The Cockapoo usually sheds its coat less than other breeds tend to do, and therefore brushing becomes more significant. This should be done on a regular basis, although the coats of puppies are less profuse than those of adults. Nevertheless, it helps to groom a young Cockapoo from an early age to get it accustomed to the experience. It will also be important for the young dog to visit a grooming parlour, where its coat can be clipped and it can be given a bath.

Preventing weight gain checklist

✓ Adhere to the on-pack instructions when feeding your dog
✓ Weigh your pet regularly, ideally by persuading it to sit on the bathroom scales for this purpose. Keep the results in a diary
✓ Monitor your pet's appearance. If you can no longer feel the ribs, your dog is probably overweight
✓ Avoid excessive use of treats, and do not feed your dog tidbits
✓ Act immediately if weight begins to increase, to avoid the situation becoming worse

A selection of tools suitable for grooming a Cockapoo. Brushes can help to remove loose hair in the coat, while combs will break down any tangles.

A young Cockapoo should be groomed to help keep its coat in healthy condition. Grooming a young dog regularly will also ensure that it doesn't resent the process when it is older.

This type of brush is especially useful for removing old hair from the coat, effectively thinning it. This is especially important since most Cockapoos do not shed regularly.

Dogs generally like being groomed, with brushing helping to improve blood circulation to the skin and creating a feeling of well-being. It will also help you establish a bond with your dog through regular, gentle contact.

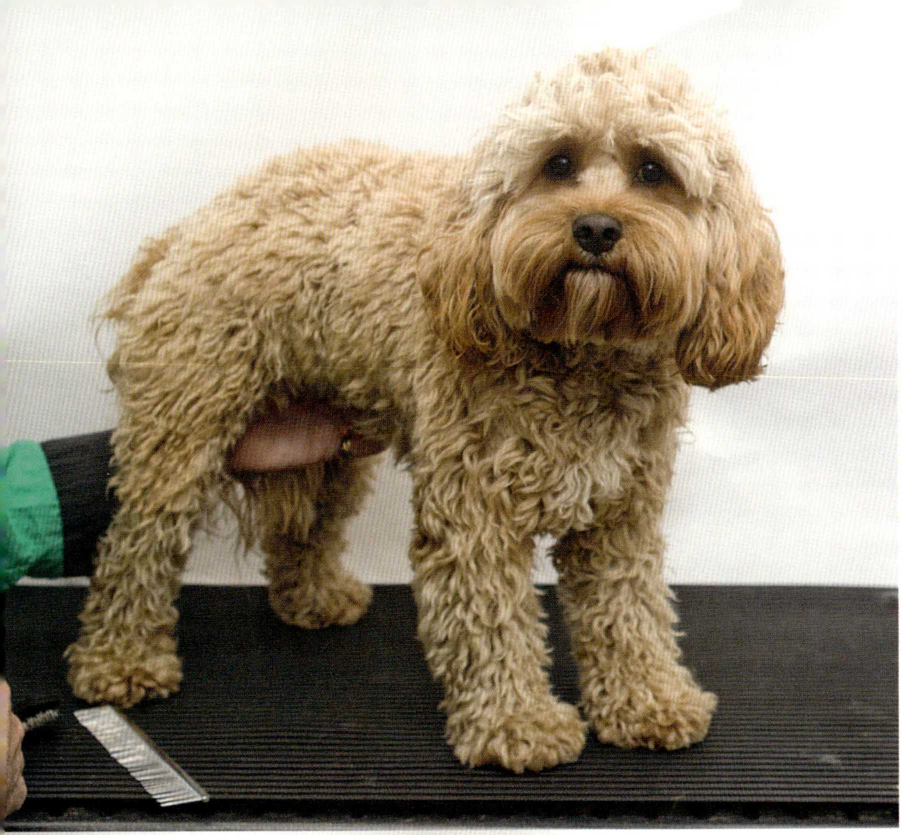

What can be achieved by professional grooming can be seen in these two 'before and after' shots, with trimming and bathing altering the Cockapoo's appearance quite markedly.

Fleas, ticks and mites

It is important to check your pet's coat while you are grooming it, since this can help you spot any parasites that may be lurking there. You are generally unlikely to see a flea, but more probably will see its dirt, which appears as tiny dark specks in the coat. This will be much easier to identify if you have a pale-coloured rather than a predominantly black Cockapoo. To check if it is indeed flea dirt, simply put some onto a piece of white paper towel and dribble a couple of spots of water over it. If it breaks down and takes on a slightly reddish hue, this confirms it is flea dirt (the red material on the paper is undigested blood). Always suspect fleas on your dog if it starts to scratch more than usual. It is important to eradicate them, because the saliva that fleas inject into the dog's body as they feed can trigger an allergic reaction. A special fine-toothed flea comb may help to catch the parasites, and it's best to groom your Cockapoo outside with this so that if any of the parasites jump off they are less likely to return to your dog.

Keep a container of water handy so you can drop in any fleas that you catch. They are most commonly found along the back, especially in the fur near the base of the tail. Fleas are also a risk to your pet's health because they can sometimes carry immature tapeworms in their bodies. If the dog should swallow an infected flea, the tapeworm is likely to end up in its intestinal tract. Treatment is also important after fleas have been found on your dog. There are products you can buy to deter fleas from becoming established in the dog's environment. Such treatment needs to be given in drop form, applied to the back of the dog's neck. It won't actually stop fleas from hitching a ride on your pet's body, but it will prevent them breeding successfully by blocking development of the flea's eggs.

In a multi-pet household it may not only be your dog that is infected. Cats can also suffer from fleas, and the parasites can transfer back and forth between your animals. It's therefore wise to treat them at the same time, though note that flea treatments for dogs are not likely to be safe for use on cats, so a separate treatment for the feline members of your household will be required.

You should also be alert to the possible presence of ticks, which your dog may sometimes acquire when walking in fields and other rural areas. Ticks anchor onto the dog's body and penetrate the skin with their powerful mouthparts, and then suck its blood. Again, ticks can cause severe irritation when they feed, and may also transmit blood parasites and other dangerous disease-causing microbes. This applies particularly in the case of Lyme disease, the symptoms of which include fever and joint pain, as well as loss of appetite. Blood tests will be necessary to confirm the diagnosis, and antibiotic treatment will then be required. (In parts of the world where this disease is prevalent, vaccination to protect against it may be possible.)

Ticks swell as they feed, sometimes reaching the size of the nail on your little finger. If you find a tick on your dog, do not be tempted to try and pull it off; you will probably leave the parasite's head parts anchored firmly in the skin where they are likely to cause an infection. Instead, there are tick-detaching sprays that you can use to persuade them to loosen their grip, not to mention special tools for this purpose. The simplest action, though, is to smear the tick's body with petroleum jelly, paying particular attention to its rear end. This should block off its breathing hole, forcing it to release its grip. There is no risk of ticks breeding on your dog.

Some parasites are more seasonal, and this applies to the harvest mite, whose larvae will affect dogs in late summer – as the name suggests. They tend to localize around the feet, causing your dog to chew very determinedly at this part of its body. You need to deal cautiously with this situation, because the irritation can be so intense that your dog may snap at you when you try to look at its feet. If the problem appears to be afflicting more than one foot, the chances are it will be these parasites that are the cause, but the situation may be more complicated if only one foot seems to be affected. You will probably need to take your Cockapoo to the vet so that it can be sedated if necessary while the cause of the problem is identified.

Claws

Grooming does not just mean coat care. You need to keep a check on the length of your Cockapoo's claws, and particularly any dewclaws (the raised claws found on the upper part of the foot, on the inside leg) that are present. Their prominent position means that they can become snagged on bushes or undergrowth, or even on fabric and suchlike, and may become torn. Because they are not in contact with the ground, dewclaws do not wear down naturally and are likely to need trimming back. There is also the possibility of them curving round into the pad behind if they grow too long. It is best to ask either your vet or groomer to trim back your Cockapoo's claws as necessary, rather than trying to do it yourself, especially if you do not have a proper pair of clippers. Also, if they are cut too short, the claws will bleed.

Eyes and ears

You may occasionally see some tear staining below the eyes, on the hair closest to the nose, most evident in Cockapoos with pale coats. It can be wiped off with a damp piece of cottonwool, although if the problem keeps recurring, seek veterinary advice in case there is an underlying eye ailment. You must also clean your pet's ears regularly.

Although less prone to ear infections than Cocker Spaniels – which have very heavy, well-furred pendulous ears that lie close to the head – Cockapoos can suffer from infections here. Repeated scratching is again a common sign of a problem, and early treatment is advised. You will need to acquire special medication from your vet, in the form of drops. Ear disease is often the result of a mixed infection, with bacteria, fungi and ear mites all commonly implicated in some cases, and effective treatment must address all three problems. As a preventative measure, however, trim back on a regular basis any fur around the entrance to the ear canal that could be causing an obstruction, and wipe around the top of the ear canal with moist cottonwool to keep the area clean. Don't probe down the ear canal, however, since this can cause injury and may even actually make an infection more likely to develop.

Other considerations

Another problem to be aware of is the possibility that your dog has acquired a sharp, pointed grass seed that has worked its way in via the foot (usually between the toes), or pad, and this will be intensely painful. This is not uncommon in the Cocker Spaniel side of a Cockapoo's family tree, for these working dogs are often out in fields and such places. Unfortunately, it can be amazingly difficult to locate a grass seed once it has entered the dog's body, because they can travel quite a distance from the point of entry. Your dog may have to be anaesthetized in order to investigate, with special forceps being used to try and retrieve the seed once its point of entry into the body has been accurately determined.

Other lumps discovered on the body while grooming your pet should be treated with suspicion, and checked out by a vet. Dogs can suffer from various skin cancers, and wart-type growths are not uncommon in older individuals especially. If these are not removed, be careful grooming around them, since they are quite vascular and may bleed readily if nicked with a metal comb, for example.

Tear-staining is especially likely to be obvious in pale-coated Cockapoos like this one, and will form a dark streak below the corner of each eye when it occurs.

Growing up

It's generally accepted that the puppy phase of a dog's life continues until six months of age, so, if you have been using a food intended for puppies, this is the point at which you should begin feeding adult dog food to your Cockapoo. Make the change gradually over the course of a week or so, increasing the amount of the new food while reducing the percentage of the puppy food, until you end up offering adult food only. It's possible that you have been buying your puppy food in large sacks. These usually represent good value for money, but if you do have one of these, make sure that you don't end up with a large amount of puppy food left over when the time for switching over arrives. Also, when buying large sacks (for puppies or for adult dogs), check the expiry date on the packaging. The nutritional value – particularly the level of vitamins in the food – may fall below its optimum level, and this is likely to have an adverse effect on your pet's health.

In bicoloured Cockapoos, the pattern of contrasting markings in their coat remains constant as they grow older.

As they mature, male Cockapoos may become more assertive and increasingly inclined to stray. Neutering can help to prevent this.

Behavioural changes

Once your Cockapoo reaches the age of six months or so, you will begin to notice behavioural signs linked to the onset of sexual maturity. In a male dog, one of the most obvious indicators will be that it lifts a hind leg to urinate; this is also the stage when a male dog may be more inclined to stray, attracted by bitches in heat, and becoming more assertive in its relations with other dogs that it encounters when out for a walk. Bitches, too, will become sexually active from about a year old and will be starting their periods of heat or 'seasons.' They will also be inclined to stray now as they, too, search for a mate, and close supervision will be necessary to prevent unwanted pregnancies.

Out and about

You are very likely to meet other dogs in local parks and other public spaces. This interaction is important, and will help to ensure that your puppy develops into a well-balanced individual that is neither nervous nor aggressive in the company of other dogs. Another way to achieve this is by taking the puppy to socialization classes (puppy parties), which many veterinary practices and dog trainers organize for clients with young dogs. You can also book classes to gain more insight into training your Cockapoo as well as addressing any particular difficulties that you have encountered. Although all dogs are individuals, the patience and time you put in as a teacher will obviously influence how quickly your own companion becomes trained.

An extending lead will be very useful, both in the garden and the park or countryside as a way of reinforcing key training lessons before allowing your puppy to run freely in public. Providing that you are walking across open ground, you can play out the lead, allowing your Cockapoo to explore further away from you without any risk of it becoming entangled in undergrowth.

Nose-to-nose. Here, a
Cockapoo meets a Whippet
and stands his ground.
Eye contact is particularly
important among dogs in
determining dominance at
such times.

Two Cockapoos meet,
with the black and white
individual approaching
the apricot dog ...

... it tries to attract the other Cockapoo's attention by sniffing in the vicinity of the ears. The other dog does not respond immediately, and feels under no threat ...

... now, the apricot Cockapoo has decided to stand up and stare at its black and white companion nose-to-nose. When meeting like this, dogs should always be allowed to get to know each other in their own way and at their own pace, rather than being forced together.

While doing this, persuade the dog to sit occasionally before calling it back to you, just as it would at home when coming for a meal. Run through the lessons that your pet has already learned. You can begin using your hands to reinforce the "Come" command as well; this may be necessary when your Cockapoo is actually running free and cannot hear your voice. Hand signals become much more important in these situations, but use them at first in conjunction with verbal commands, so that your dog comes to associate the sound and movement together. Another method of getting your dog to respond to the

The apricot Cockapoo has adopted a play bow stance, expecting the other Cockapoo to take up its invitation.

The apricot Cockapoo has now picked up the ball and is being chased by the other dog.

Mixing with other dogs is strongly recommended for Cockapoos once they have completed their course of vaccinations. This makes them less nervous.

Encourage your Cockapoo to run when it is off the lead, since this will help to maintain general fitness – and it's fun!

command is to use an ultrasonic dog whistle, the sound frequency of which is much too high for us to hear, but is well within the canine audible range. You must devise your own whistling pattern – perhaps two short blasts followed by a long one – which your Cockapoo will come to identify with in due course. This will be vital in maintaining communication if your dog disappears in woodland, for example.

Off the lead

When you feel confident enough to let your Cockapoo off the lead, you may find that it doesn't stray very far at first. However, once the dog has become used to being off the lead and is a little more confident, it may venture out of sight. Occupying the dog's attention by throwing a toy such as a Frisbee for it to chase and retrieve may help to reduce the risk of this happening. It will also give the young dog more exercise as it runs back and forth.

If your dog gets particularly wet and muddy after a walk you may need to bath it. Depending on the size of your dog, a plastic baby bath will be useful for this purpose. You can simply wash the dog first with a special canine shampoo, taking great care not to let any enter the eyes. Then tip this water away, and rinse the coat thoroughly using a measuring jug to pour clean tepid water over your pet's back. Another option is to put the animal in the bath (with a bath mat to stand on) and use the shower attachment. Afterwards, the dog will shake much of the water out of its coat, and you can dry it with a towel. Don't let your dog get cold and begin to shiver; use a hairdryer to dry the coat thoroughly.

Neutering

One of the best ways to lessen the risk of your Cockapoo being involved in a serious fight is by neutering, particularly in the case of a male dog. Neutering will also result in a cessation of signs of sexual behaviour, and has another

When first off the lead, the young Cockapoo will begin to investigate its surroundings by having a thorough sniff around. Don't let it stray too far until you are confident that it will return to you when called.

Chasing a ball helps the Cockapoo to replicate part of its natural activity, plus keep your dog fit and relatively warm on a cold day.

significant advantage in terms of decreasing the likelihood that your pet will stray. Known as castration, this surgery involves the removal of both testes.

The equivalent type of surgery in a bitch is known as spaying, and involves removal of the ovaries and uterus. Spaying will prevent any subsequent periods of 'heat' that will otherwise typically occur every six months, when the bitch is likely to become sexually active. Male dogs will almost inevitably pursue her at this stage, as she releases chemical messengers – called pheromones – that are wafted in the air. Even in very minute concentrations, these are still strong enough to attract potential mates from a wide area. Also, by removing the uterus, there is no risk that the bitch may succumb to an infection of the womb called pyometra. This is one of the major illnesses affecting the female's reproductive tract. Spaying also eliminates false pregnancies, which can even result in the production of milk about nine weeks after the last period of heat, around the time when puppies would normally be born.

If your bitch is not neutered, you should not take her out for a walk when she is in season, since she will almost certainly end up mating. Dogs will mate indiscriminately, so any intact male dog can sire a litter of puppies.

Hazards outside the home

Other potential dangers exist which you may encounter when walking with your dog; another reason why it is important to have good control over your pet at all times. Be wary when you are walking near water, particularly rivers, in case your puppy decides to jump in and cannot get out again. Ponds and lakes can become particularly dangerous in winter, too, especially if it is icy. A dog's weight may well be sufficient to break the ice on the surface of a lake or pond, even if it seems thick enough at the margins, plunging the animal into the freezing water beneath.

On beaches where dogs are permitted, beware of the risk of your pet slipping into quicksand, or being swept out to sea by a strong current. Cliff edges can also be dangerous places for dogs. Always err on the side of caution, therefore, and put your dog on a lead if there is a possibility of danger. This certainly applies when you are close to livestock such as horses and also cows. The latter, in particular, are likely to resent the presence of a dog in their midst, particularly if they have calves. Dogs may also chase or even attack sheep, especially lambing ewes, and so must be kept on a lead at all times when in their vicinity.

Luckily in Britain and much of mainland Europe there is only one venomous snake – the Adder – and none at all in Ireland. However, this is by no means the case in other parts of the world, where there are not just venomous snakes but

Warning!

If your dog goes into water, do not wade in after it, especially if it has gone into a river. Sadly, people are drowned every year trying to rescue their pets in this type of situation. The chances are that the dog will be able to swim better than you, and the best course of action instead is to call the Cockapoo. Hopefully, it will swim to the bank, from where you can help it onto dry land. The situation will be even more dangerous if the water is frozen. Ice may well support your dog's weight, but not yours should you try to follow it. Even if the ice at the edge of the water supports your dog's weight, it may be thinner further out in the middle. As always, therefore, plan ahead for possible danger when taking your dog out, and follow either a different route or put your pet back on its lead at an early stage if there is a potential hazard ahead.

Be very careful when your Cockapoo is close to water, especially given the poodle's passion for working in this type of environment.

also powerful constrictor snakes that can easily overpower a Border Terrier. In Britain, dogs usually suffer snake bites from spring until autumn, especially in heathland where Adders tend to live. You are unlikely to see the snake, but the curiosity of a young puppy can lead it into danger. Should you find that your pet suddenly becomes weak and has difficulty walking, the likelihood is that it may have been bitten, in which case you should pick it up and seek veterinary help as soon as possible.

Holiday time

Whether you are holidaying at home or abroad, it is important to make any necessary plans for your pet well in advance. If you are travelling abroad it is now sometimes possible to take your dog with you, depending on where you live and where you are going. There are some dog-friendly hotels where you can stay with your pet at a modest extra cost. However, some establishments will not let you leave your Cockapoo on its own in the room while you go out. You will also be responsible for any damage caused by your pet.

Taking your dog on a touring holiday is not such a good idea, because this will entail a lot of travelling. Furthermore, if you want to go somewhere that does not accept dogs, such as a restaurant, that may not be possible because you should not leave your pet on its own in the car. This is particularly ill advised during the summer, when the temperature inside a parked vehicle can rise to a fatal level within minutes. Simply leaving the windows wound down slightly will not be sufficient; sadly, every year dogs die in cars all over the world because their owners do not appreciate the danger. You could even find yourself prosecuted if you

You can travel from the UK to other parts of Europe with your pet under what is popularly known as the Pet Passport Scheme, although the scheme is officially described as the Pet Travel Scheme. Full details of the requirements (which can change from time to time) are to be found on the DEFRA website.

Basically, your dog must be vaccinated against the killer disease rabies, in addition to being microchipped, and will also need to be treated against parasites before returning to the UK. You also need to be certain that the journey itself will not be upsetting for your terrier, and that the whole experience will be better than leaving your pet at home. It is perhaps worth remembering that there is a slightly increased risk of your dog succumbing to other 'exotic' diseases – such as leishmaniasis and heartworm – that cannot be guarded against by vaccination, and yet thrive in warmer areas outside Britain.

If you decide not to take your pet, various other options exist. One possibility is to book a home-sitting service to look after your pet in your home. Most home-sitters are retired people who have expertise in looking after animals, but always take up the references of the company concerned before confirming a booking. It is also advisable to contact your insurer to check that you will not be invalidating your cover. Using this type of service also means that your home will not be left empty while you are away. It is likely to be a cost-effective (and convenient) choice if you have a menagerie of creatures, which would otherwise need to be boarded out in your absence.

Kennels

The most obvious choice of holiday care for your dog is a boarding kennel. It pays to check out the establishment first, though, to be sure you are happy with the standard of care on offer. Start, if you can, by getting recommendations from dog-owning friends, and then contact the kennels in question to arrange a visit. It is not just cleanliness that is important, but also the general standard of accommodation. For example, will your dog be sharing a kennel and run with another dog? And are there any facilities for safe exercise out of the kennel? Perhaps the most significant factor overall will be the attitude of the staff. Small things can be good indicators. When you are being shown around, do they refer to the resident dogs by name and seem genuinely interested in them?

Try to arrange accommodation for your dog as far in advance as possible, and get this confirmed before you make your own holiday booking. Good kennels receive regular repeat bookings, and particularly at peak holiday times have very little spare accommodation.

It is advisable to arrange a vaccination to protect against kennel cough, because this illness spreads very rapidly, even in well-run establishments. It can prove debilitating, especially for older dogs. You will also need to check that your Cockapoo's other vaccinations are up to date, and that you have the vaccination certificate available (which you will need to take to the kennels). Do not leave this until the last minute, because if you find that you have mislaid the documentation you will need to get a copy from your vet.

Pack a favourite toy and a blanket to help your pet settle in your absence. You also need to provide details of your vet, and how you can be contacted in the event of an emergency. If your dog has any particular medical needs, which you should make clear at the time of booking, do not forget to hand over this medication to the kennel staff, ensuring that there is sufficient to last for the duration of your dog's stay, and that the staff are quite clear how to administer it.

It is quite usual for a dog to sense the change of routine that occurs prior to a holiday, and it may be better to book your pet in a day or two before you leave. You can then be confident that everything is sorted out, and that your dog is settled in its temporary home. Dogs will normally adjust rapidly to such surroundings, and will not mope, although you can be sure of a warm, enthusiastic welcome when you arrive home!

Home-sitting

Services of this type have become increasing popular over recent years, as an alternative to kennelling. A home-sitter, typically a retired person with considerable experience of animals, will stay in your home in your absence, and take care not only of your dog but also any other pets you may have. Clearly, this will be far less disruptive for your pet, and in this sense it is particularly valuable in the case of elderly dogs, or those suffering from chronic medical conditions that require a stable routine and regular medication. If you have a relatively large menagerie of animals of all types, it can also be cost-effective.

Only use the services of a reputable home-sitting service, though, and ask for references. Most will go to great lengths to carefully match the expertise of their personnel with the needs of their clients, but, as with boarding kennels, it is advisable to book early. It is also best to try to introduce your Cockapoo in advance to the person who will be looking after it. Run through all the relevant aspects of your dog's care when the home-sitter arrives, mentioning points such as feeding times, where the dog sleeps, daily routine, games it likes to play, and so on. It's also worth providing a written-up list of these and other particularly important in terms, including, of course, your contact details and those of your vet.

Introducing a companion

There may come a time when you decide that you want to introduce another dog into your home. Whether or not this is a Cockapoo, the same rules apply. Start by allowing the dogs to meet each other on neutral territory, in a park, for example, to reduce the risk of conflict. You will need a separate set of feeding dishes for your new pet, because mealtimes represent a potential flashpoint when two dogs are together, and, initially at least, they should be fed separately, in different parts of your home, to prevent one stealing the other's food. It is often much easier to introduce a young puppy alongside an older dog, since each has a clearly defined status, with the younger dog adopting a subordinate role. The Cockapoo's genial nature thankfully means that introductions rarely prove difficult.

There is no doubt that an introduction of this type can help rejuvenate an older dog, and, whilst never replacing an old companion, can ease the pain of its death when this happens.

Once the dogs have settled down and become well acquainted, they can have their meals alongside each other. But beware in case one eats faster and then tries to steal the other's food!

Old age

It's a sad fact that dogs have relatively short lives on average, but, thanks to advances in health care and a better appreciation of their nutritional needs, they are living longer than ever before. Although a dog like a Cockapoo becomes a 'senior' at about seven or eight years of age, with the right sort of diet and exercise, its lifespan could turn out to be double this length. Taking an older dog for regular veterinary checks every six months will also play a part in keeping your pet healthy and active. While illnesses linked with old age – such as heart disease – may not be curable, early diagnosis and treatment does mean that it is often possible to stabilize such conditions quite effectively, maintaining the dog's quality of life.

Ultimately, however, there will come a stage when your companion's quality of life has deteriorated markedly. It is always a very difficult decision to make, but when the time has come for your cherished dog to be put to sleep, you can rely on the sympathetic and professional support of your vet. Afterwards, you will probably feel that you could never have another dog, and certainly not another Cockapoo. Time is a great healer, though, and in due course you may decide that you do want another dog. As you look back over your Cockapoo's life, it will be easier to appreciate that your dog was an individual – and another Cockapoo will have its own unique personality. Another Cockapoo may even look different: as we have seen, they come in a variety of sizes, colours and coat types. Before you know it, you may be sharing your life with another of these endearing dogs.

Visit Hubble and Hattie on the web: www.hubbleandhattie.com and
www.hubbleandhattie.blogspot.com
Details of all books • New book news • Special offers

Further resources

Bibliography

Cockapoos Amon, Erin (Barron's Educational Series, 2010)
American Cocker Spaniel Beauchamp, Richard G (Interpet Publishing, 2003)
Poodle: A Comprehensive Guide to Owning and Caring for Your Dog Clark, S Meyer (Kennel Club Books, 2003)
Cockapoo: Comprehensive Owner's Guide Foley, Mary (Kennel Club Books, 2006)
Designer Dogs: Animal Planet™ Gagne, Tammy Pet Care Library (TFH, 2008)
Pet Owner's Guide to Cocker Spaniels Kane, Frank (Ringpress Books, 1999)
The Popular Cocker Spaniel Lloyd, H S (Read Books, 2007, classic reprint)

Cockapoo Club of America

http://www.cockapooclub.com

Author's website

Pet Info Club http://www.petinfoclub.com

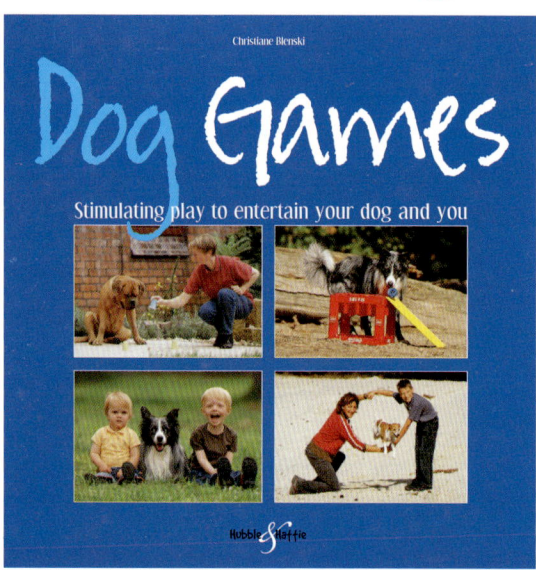

£15.99 978-1-845843-32-8

£9.99 978-1-845843-13-7

£14.99 978-1-845843-33-5

£12.99 978-1-845843-22-9

and Hattie books!

£9.99 978-1-845842-91-8

£9.99 978-1-845842-93-2

£12.99 978-1-845842-92-5

£9.99 978-1-845842-74-1

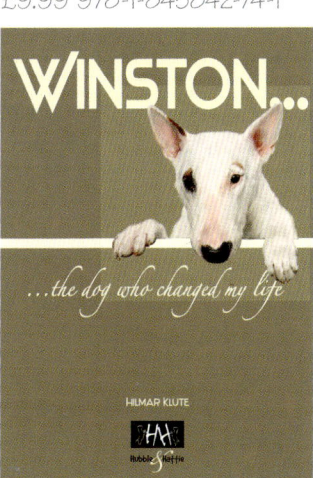

£9.99 978-1-845843-19-9

Index